BEGINNING GAMES

Alphabet Soup

Matching Games for the Alphabet

by Marilynn G. Barr

LAB201310
Beginning Games
ALPHABET SOUP
by Marilynn G. Barr

Published by: Little Acorn Books™
Originally published by: Monday Morning Books, Inc.

Entire contents copyright © 2014 Little Acorn Books™

Little Acorn Books
PO Box 8787
Greensboro, NC 27419-0787

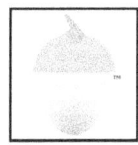

Promoting Early Skills for a Lifetime™

Little Acorn Books™
is an imprint of Little Acorn Associates, Inc.

http://www.littleacornbooks.com

Permission is hereby granted to reproduce student materials in this book for non-commercial individual or classroom use. *School-wide or system-wide use is expressly prohibited.

ISBN 978-1-937257-45-3

Printed in the United States of America

Alphabet Soup

Contents

Introduction 4	Strawberry Shortcake 39
Swing on a Star 5	Cover 40
Game Board 6	Game Board 41
Game Cards 8	Shortcake Patterns 42
Cover 9	Game Cards 45
Porcupine Cave 10	Alphabet Bowling 46
Cover 11	Cover 47
Game Board 12	Game Board 48
Game Cards 14	Bowling Pin Patterns 49
Alphabet Soup 15	Game Cards 50
Game Board 16	Zoom Zoom 51
Game Cards 18	Cover 52
Cover 19	Game Board 53
Top Hat Frogs 20	Martian Patterns 54
Game Board 21	Game Cards 56
Top Hat Frog Patterns 22	ABC Block Stackers 57
Game Cards 23	Game Board 58
Yarn Ball Fun 25	Game Cards 60
Game Board 26	
Kitten Patterns 27	
Game Cards 28	
Flower Power 30	
Game Board 31	
Flower Patterns 32	
Game Cards 33	

Alphabet Soup

Introduction

Reinforce alphabet skills with the ready-to-use beginning games featured in *Alphabet Soup*. Children practice recognizing the letters and matching pictures as they play trail, match boards, clothespin, and stacker games. Every game includes a game board and programmed playing pieces. Game formats also offer following directions, fair-play, fine-motor, and memory skills practice.

Children match uppercase and lowercase letters as they move pawns along the Porcupine Cave, Swing on a Star, and Alphabet Soup trail games. Flower Power, Yarn Ball Fun, and Top Hat Frogs clothespin games offer additional alphabet skills practice as well as fine motor skills development. Children clip clothespin game cards to flowers, playful kittens, and frogs wearing top hats. Children match letters to alphabet pictures as they play Zoom Zoom, Alphabet Bowling, and Strawberry Shortcake match board games. ABC Block Stackers offers self-checking multi-dimensional skills practice as children identify and stack matching block game cards. Long and short vowel picture cards are also provided.

Alphabet Soup Tic-Tac-Toe For Two Players

Children develop visualization and strategy skills as they play tic-tac-toe. Reproduce, color, laminate, and cut apart the game board and cards. Each player chooses the X or O cards. In turn, each player places a card on one of the tic-tac-toe spaces. The first player with three Xs or Os in a row, vertically, horizontally, or diagonally, wins.

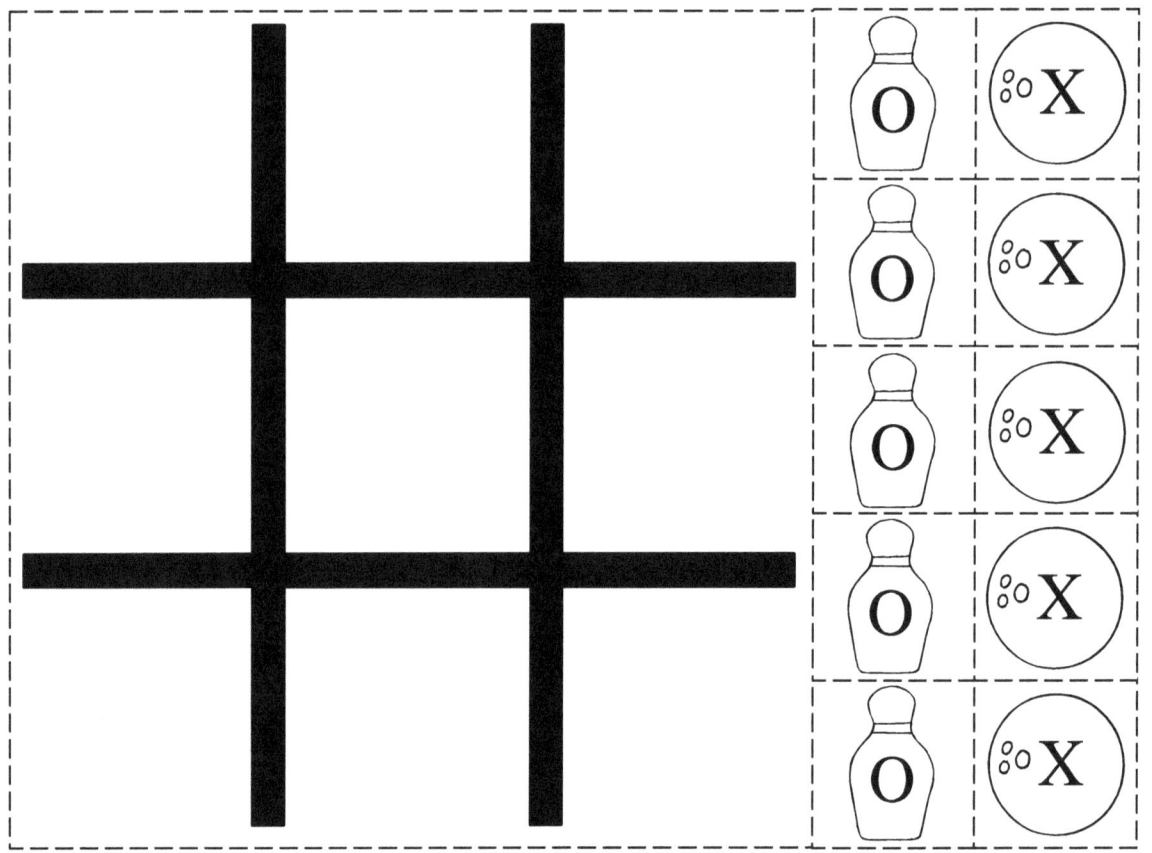

Swing on a Star
A Trail Game
For Two to Four Players

Pawns

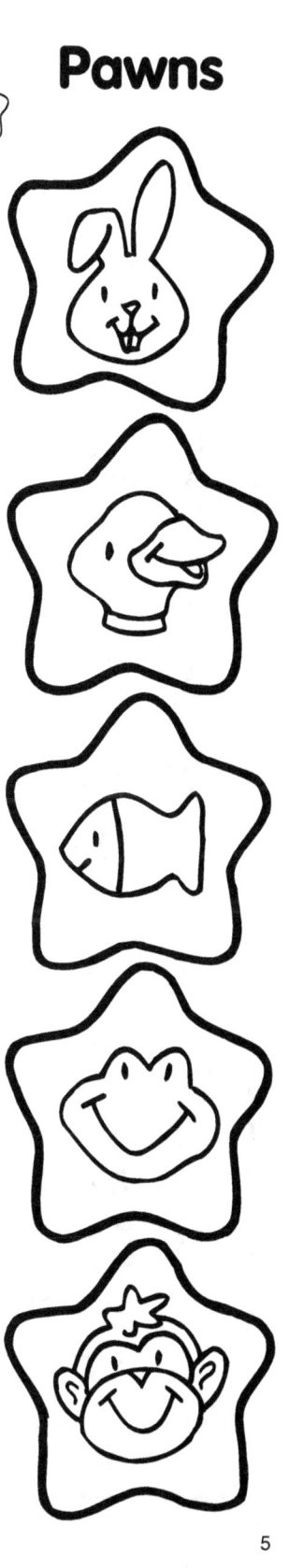

Materials

crayons, markers, scissors, glue, file folder, envelope, tape

Assembly

Game Board: Reproduce, color, and cut out the cover and game board patterns. Matching in the center, glue the game board patterns to the inside of a folder. Glue the cover to the front of the folder, then laminate. Tape an envelope to the back of the game board folder to store pawns and game cards.

Pawns: Reproduce, color, laminate, and cut out a set of pawns. Store the pawns in the envelope on the back of the folder.

Game Cards: Reproduce, color, laminate, then cut out the game cards. Option: Reproduce, color, and glue each page of cards to the back of a sheet of gift wrap, then laminate and cut out the cards. Store the game cards in the envelope on the back of the game board folder.

How to Play

Set up the game board and cards on a table. Each player chooses a pawn. Then one player shuffles and places the deck of cards, face down, on the table. Each player, in turn, draws a card and moves his or her pawn to the next matching space on the game board. Drawn cards are placed, face down, in a discard pile. Play continues until each player reaches the swinging star at The End. When all the cards have been drawn, reshuffle the discard pile and continue playing.

Swing on a Star Game Board

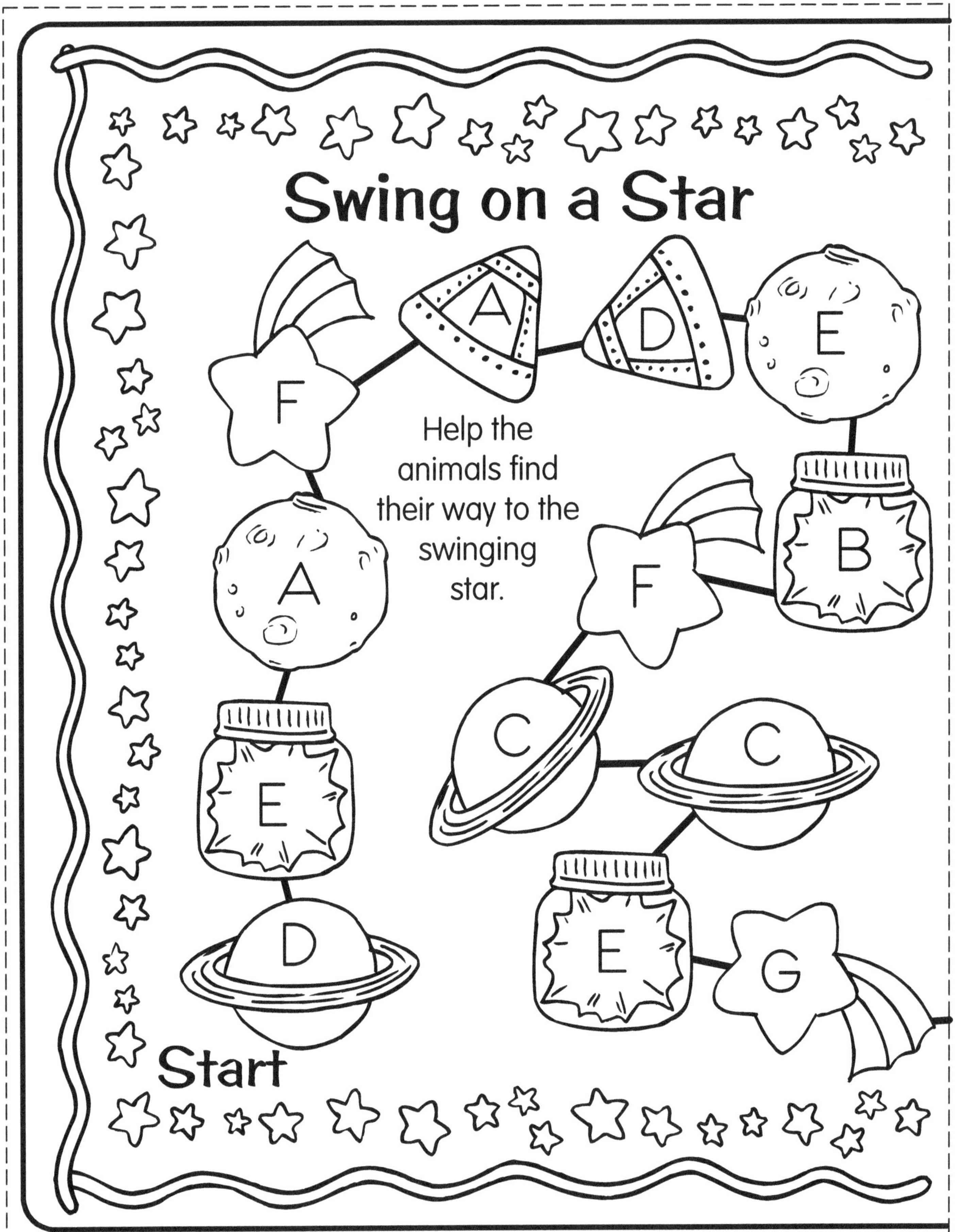

Swing on a Star
Help the animals find their way to the swinging star.
Start
D
E
A
F
A
D
E
B
F
C
C
E
G

LAB201310 • ALPHABET SOUP • 978-1-937257-45-3 •

Swing on a Star Game Board

Star Game Cards

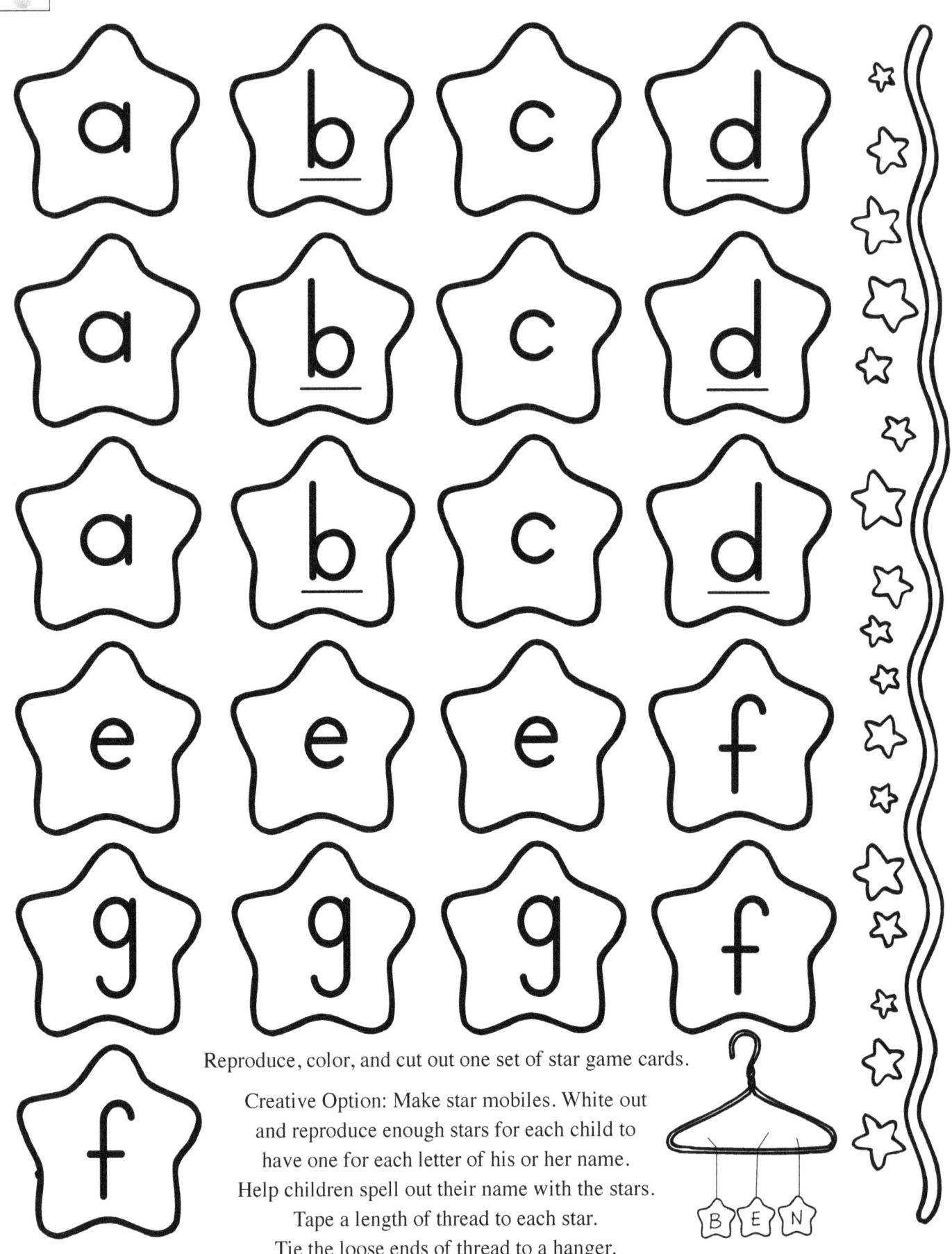

Reproduce, color, and cut out one set of star game cards.

Creative Option: Make star mobiles. White out and reproduce enough stars for each child to have one for each letter of his or her name. Help children spell out their name with the stars. Tape a length of thread to each star. Tie the loose ends of thread to a hanger.

Swing on a Star Cover

Porcupine Cave
A Trail Game
For Two to Four Players

Materials
crayons, markers, scissors, glue, file folder, envelope, tape

Assembly
Game Board: Reproduce, color, and cut out the cover and game board patterns. Matching in the center, glue the game board patterns to the inside of a folder. Glue the cover to the front of the folder, then laminate. Tape an envelope to the back of the game board folder to store pawns and game cards.

Pawns: Reproduce, color, laminate, and cut out a set of pawns. Store the pawns in the envelope on the back of the folder.

Game Cards: Reproduce, color, laminate, then cut out the game cards. Option: Reproduce, color, and glue the game cards page to the back of a sheet of gift wrap, then laminate and cut out the cards. Store the game cards in the envelope on the back of the game board folder.

How to Play
Set up the game board and cards on a table. Each player chooses a pawn. Then one player shuffles and places the log game cards, face down, on the table. Each player, in turn, draws a card and moves his or her pawn to the next matching space on the game board. Drawn cards are placed, face down, in a discard pile. Play continues until each player reaches the cave at The End. When all the cards have been drawn, reshuffle the discard pile and continue playing.

Pawns

Porcupine Cave Cover

Porcupine Cave

Porcupine Cave Game Board

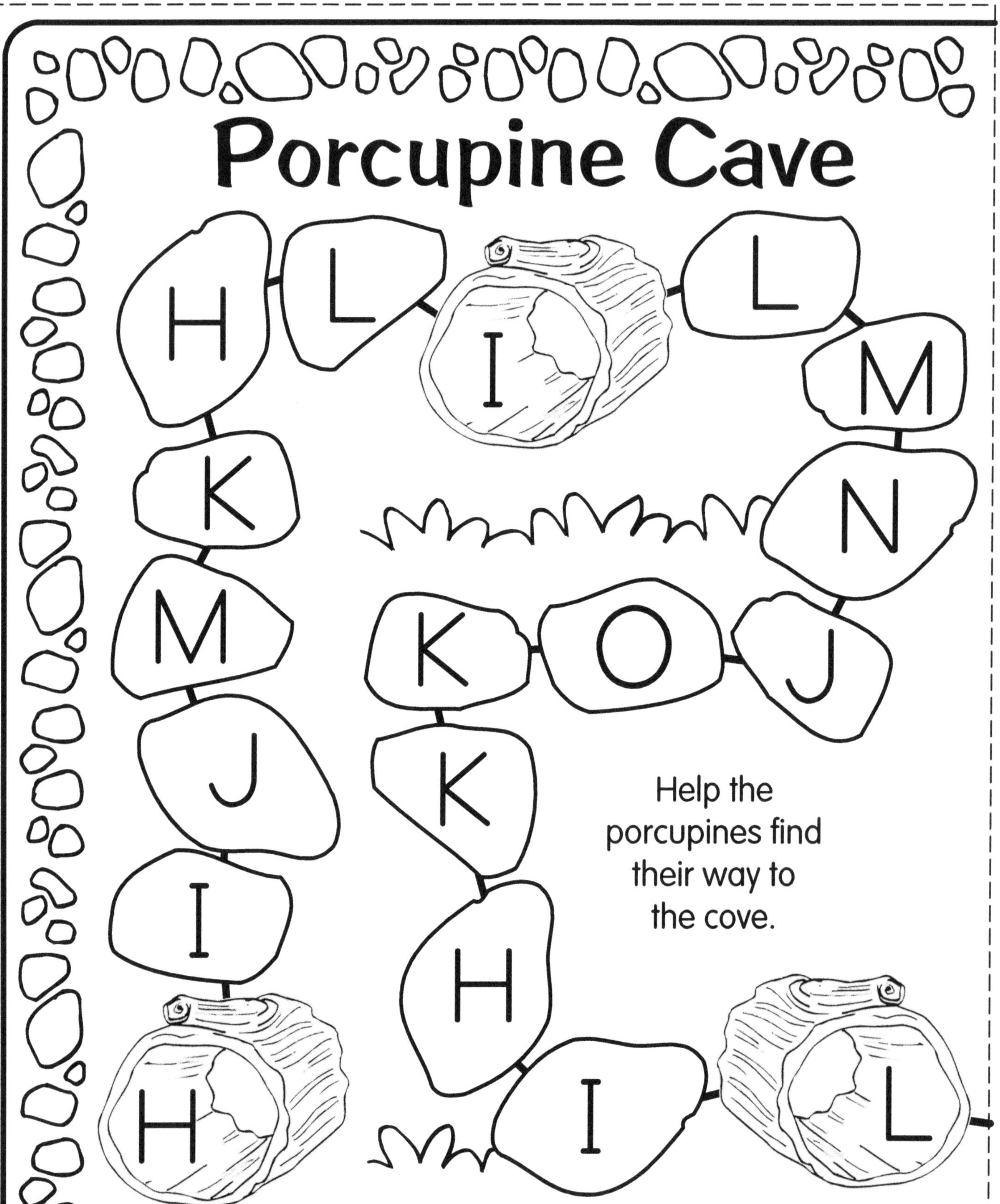

Porcupine Cave

H L I L M
K N
M K O J
J
I K
H
H I L

Help the porcupines find their way to the cove.

Start

Porcupine Cave Game Board

Log Game Cards

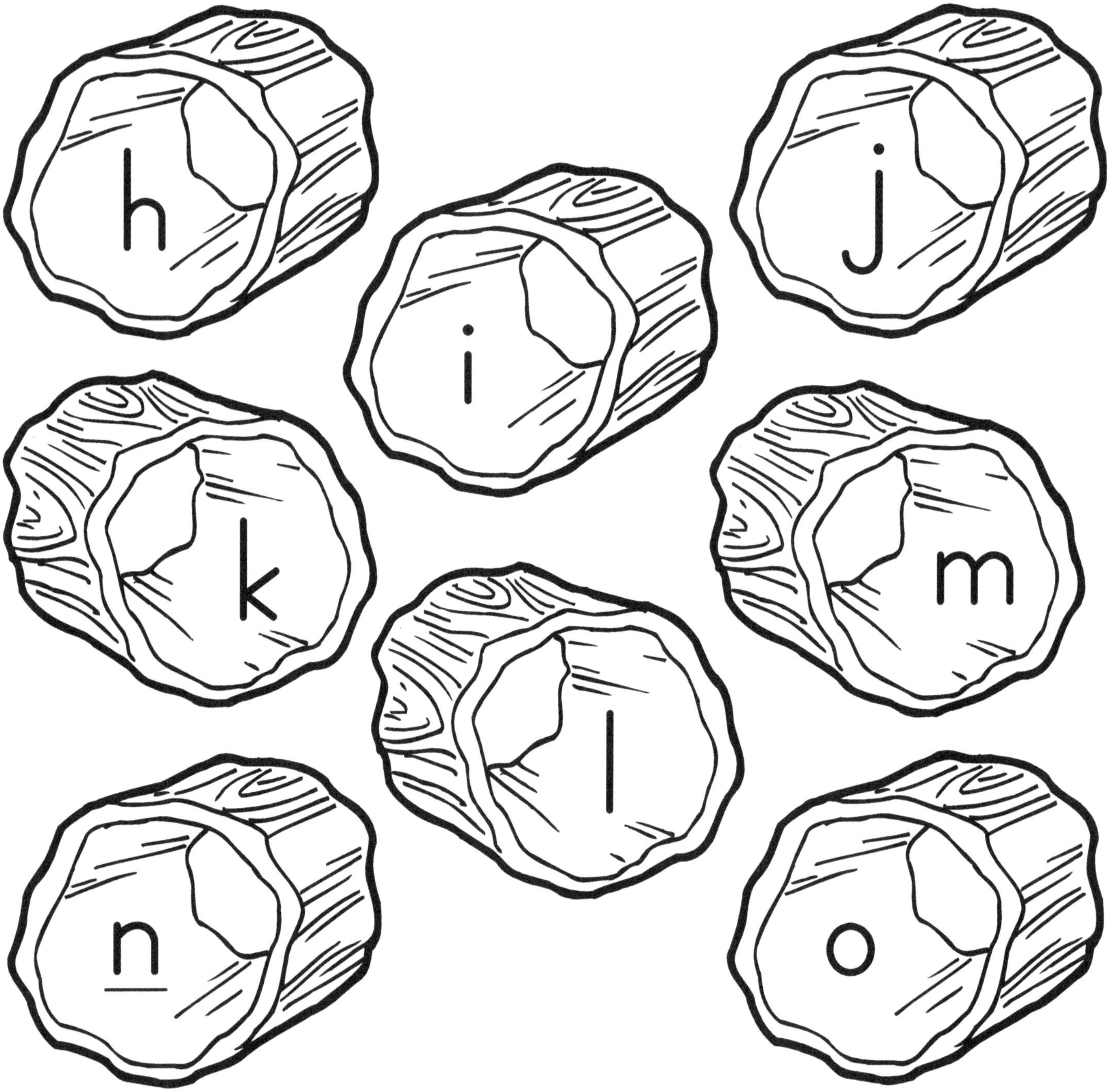

h j i k m l n o

Reproduce, color, and cut out two sets of log game cards.

Creative Option: Reproduce a set of log game cards for each child to color and cut out.
Have children cut out and glue pictures of creatures from nature magazines on each log.
Then help each child arrange and glue his or her creature logs on a sheet of construction paper.
Children can add details such as grass, bushes, cards trees to their pictures.

Alphabet Soup
A Trail Game
For Two to Four Players

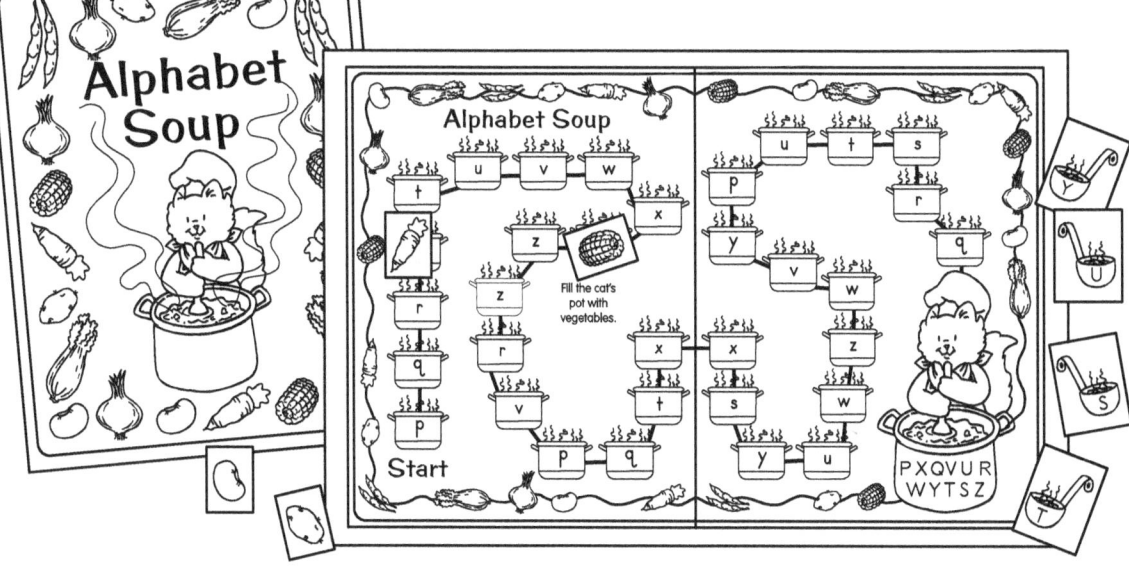

Pawns

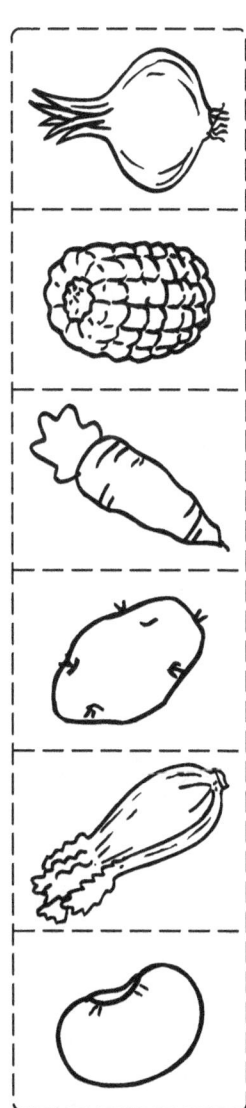

Materials
crayons, markers, scissors, glue, file folder, envelope, tape

Assembly
Game Board: Reproduce, color, and cut out the cover and game board patterns. Matching in the center, glue the game board patterns to the inside of a folder. Glue the cover to the front of the folder, then laminate. Tape an envelope to the back of the game board folder to store pawns and game cards.

Pawns: Reproduce, color, laminate, and cut out a set of pawns. Store the pawns in the envelope on the back of the folder.

Game Cards: Reproduce, color, laminate, then cut apart the game cards. Option: Reproduce, color, and glue each page of cards to the back of a sheet of gift wrap, then laminate and cut apart the cards. Store the game cards in the envelope on the back of the game board folder.

How to Play
Set up the game board and cards on a table. Each player chooses a pawn. Then one player shuffles and places the deck of cards, face down, on the table. Each player, in turn, draws a card and moves his or her pawn to the next matching space on the game board. Drawn cards are placed, face down, in a discard pile. Play continues until each player reaches the soup pot at the end. When all the cards have been drawn, reshuffle the discard pile and continue playing.

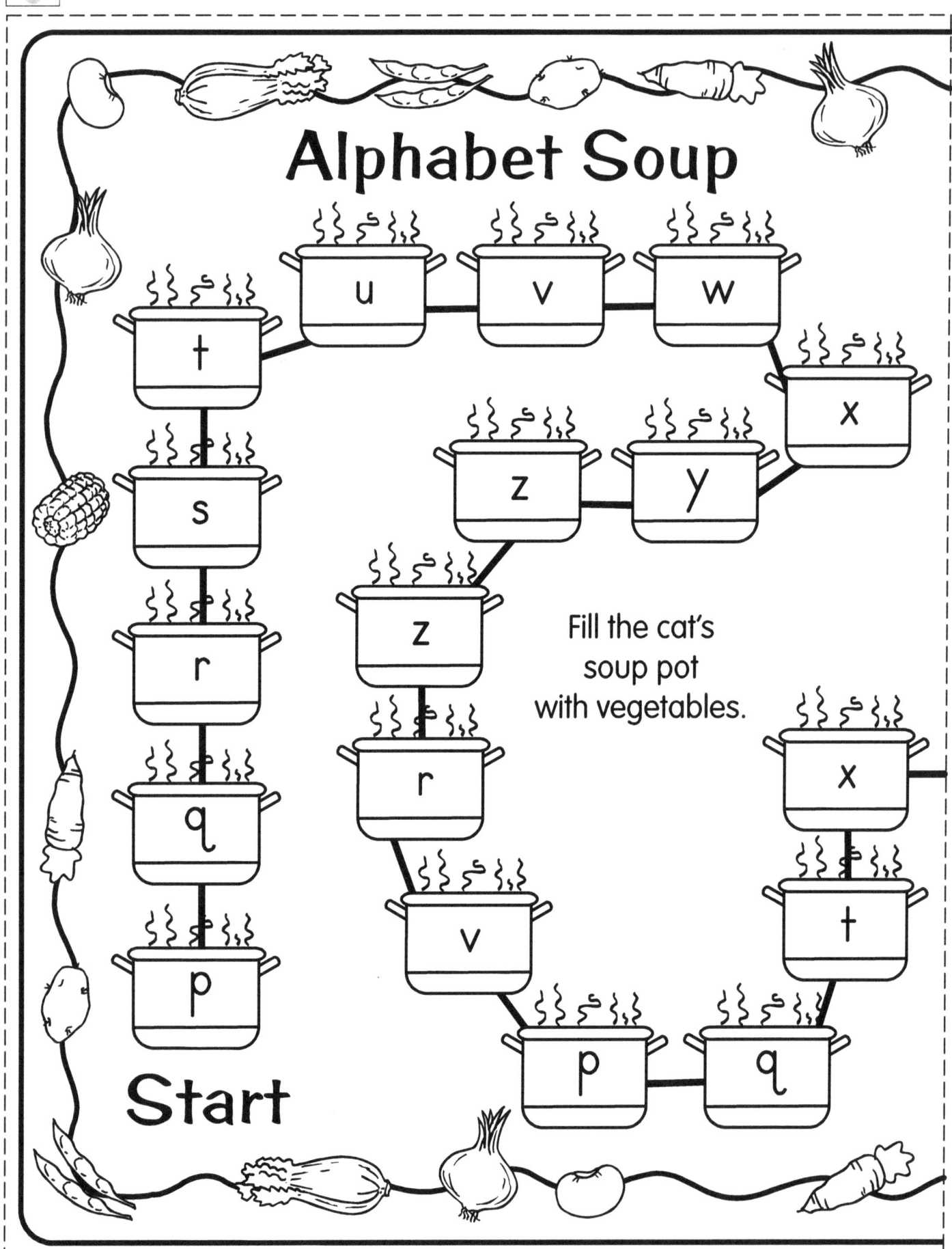

Alphabet Soup Game Board

Ladle Game Cards

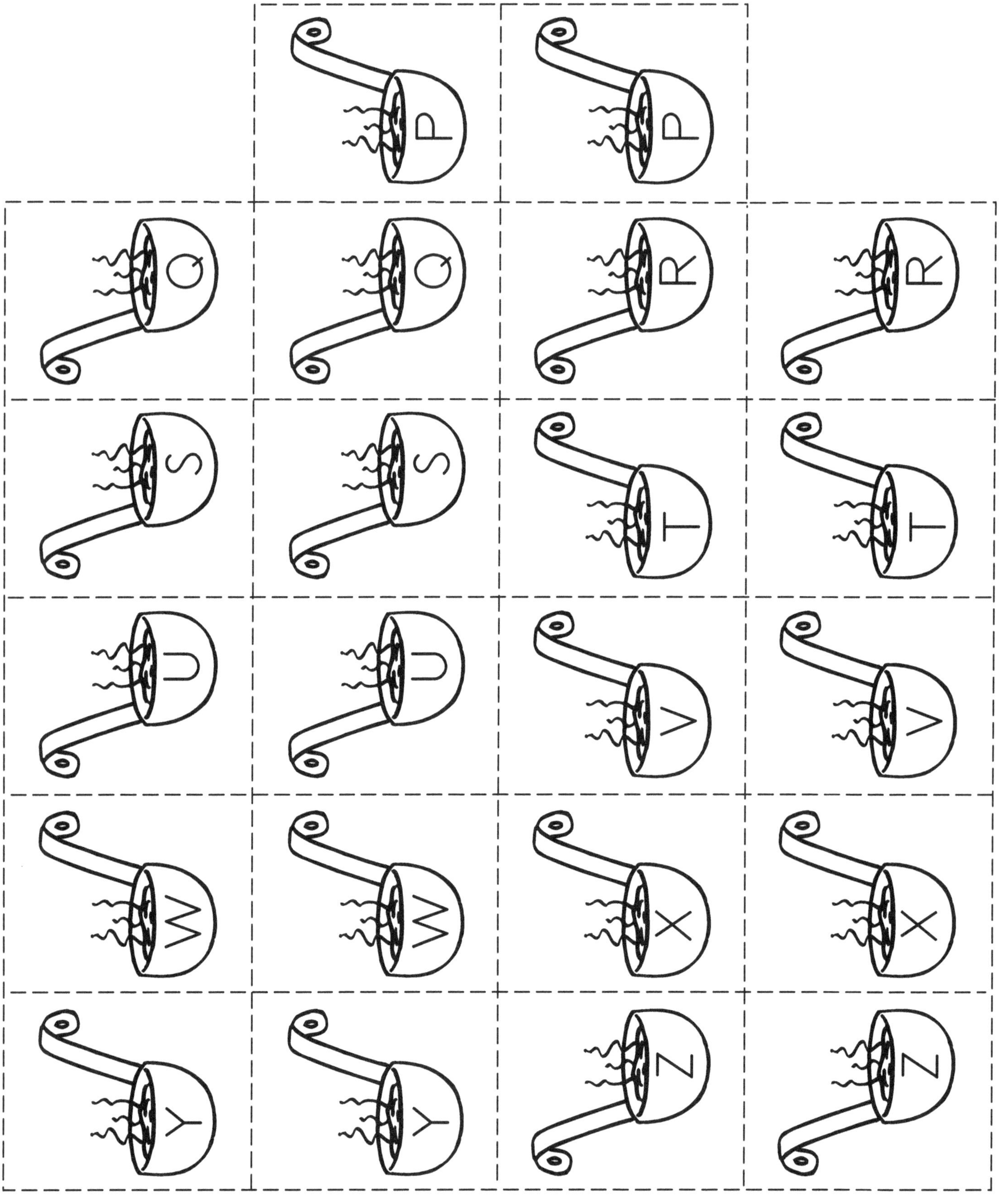

Reproduce, color, laminate, then cut apart one set of game cards.

Alphabet Soup Cover

Alphabet Soup

Top Hat Frogs
A Clothespin Game
For Two Players

Materials
crayons, markers, scissors, glue, file folders, clothespins, large envelope

Assembly
Game Board: Reproduce, color, and cut out four game board patterns. Matching along the straight edges, glue the game board patterns on a poster board circle to form a round game board. Glue the title in the center of the game board. Reproduce two sets of frog patterns. Reproduce, color, cut out, and glue an alphabet picture game card on each frog pattern. Then glue the frog patterns around the game board. Note: Make additional game boards to provide skills practice for the entire alphabet.

Clothespin Game Cards: Reproduce, color, and cut out eight uppercase letter game cards to match the alphabet pictures on the game board. Glue a clothespin to the back of each game card. Decorate a large envelope with frog and top hat cutouts. Store the clothespin game cards in the envelope. (Include non-matching game cards for advanced players, or all matches for early learners.)

How to Play
Set up the game board on a table. Place the clothespin game cards, face down, on the table. Each player, in turn, draws a clothespin. If there is a match, the player identifies the match, and clips the clothespin to the correct space. If there is no match, the player places the clothespin back on the table, face down. Play continues until a clothespin is attached to each matching frog on the game board.

Top Hat Frogs Game Board and Title

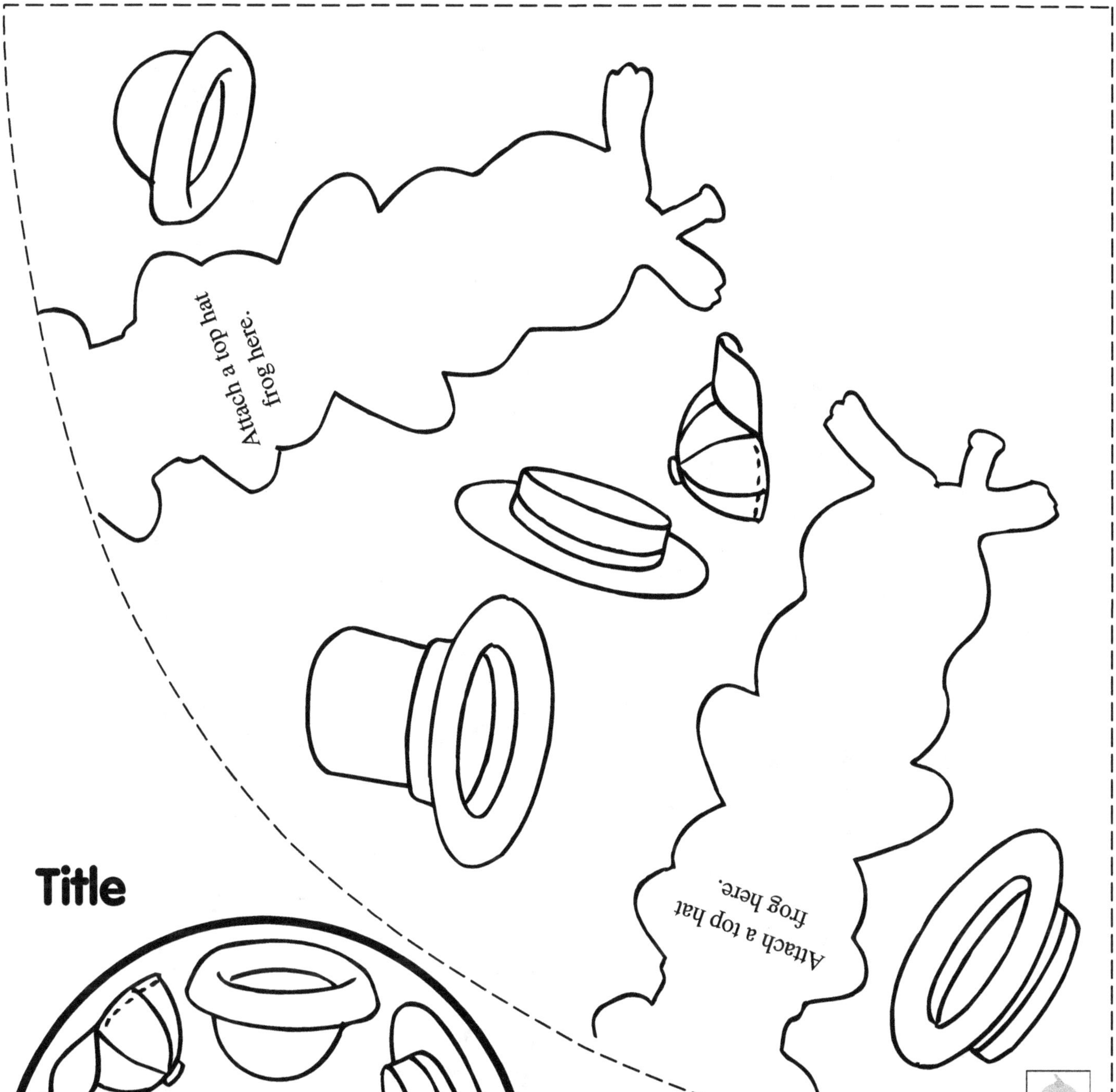

Attach a top hat frog here.

Attach a top hat frog here.

Title

Top Hat Frogs

Reproduce, color, cut out, and assemble four game board patterns on a poster board circle to form a round game board. Glue the title in the center of the game board.

Top Hat Frog Patterns

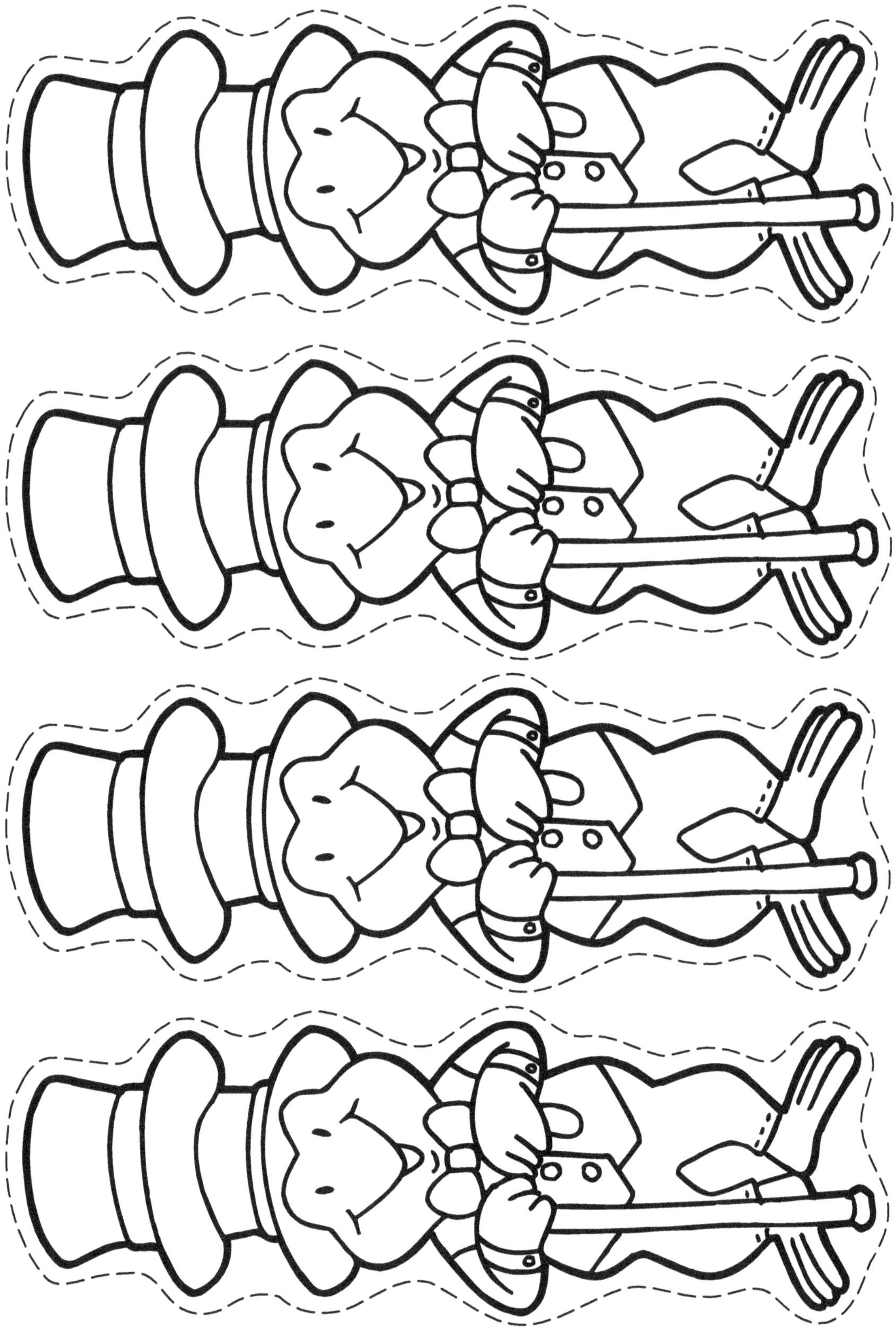

Reproduce two sets of frog patterns.

Creative Option: Reproduce, color, and cut out oak tag frog patterns.
Tape or glue a craft stick to the back of each frog to form a stick puppet.

Top Hat Game Cards

Reproduce, color, cut out, and glue an alphabet picture game card on each frog pattern. Then glue the frog patterns around an assembled Top Hat Frogs game board. Note: Make additional game boards to provide skills practice for the entire alphabet.

Top Hat Game Cards

A B C D E F G
H I J K L M N
O P Q R S T U
V W X Y Z

Creative Option: Reproduce, color, cut out, and glue two sets of alphabet picture or uppercase letter top hat game cards on round, colored construction paper circles for children to play a game of Concentration.

Yarn Ball Fun
A Clothespin Game
For Two Players

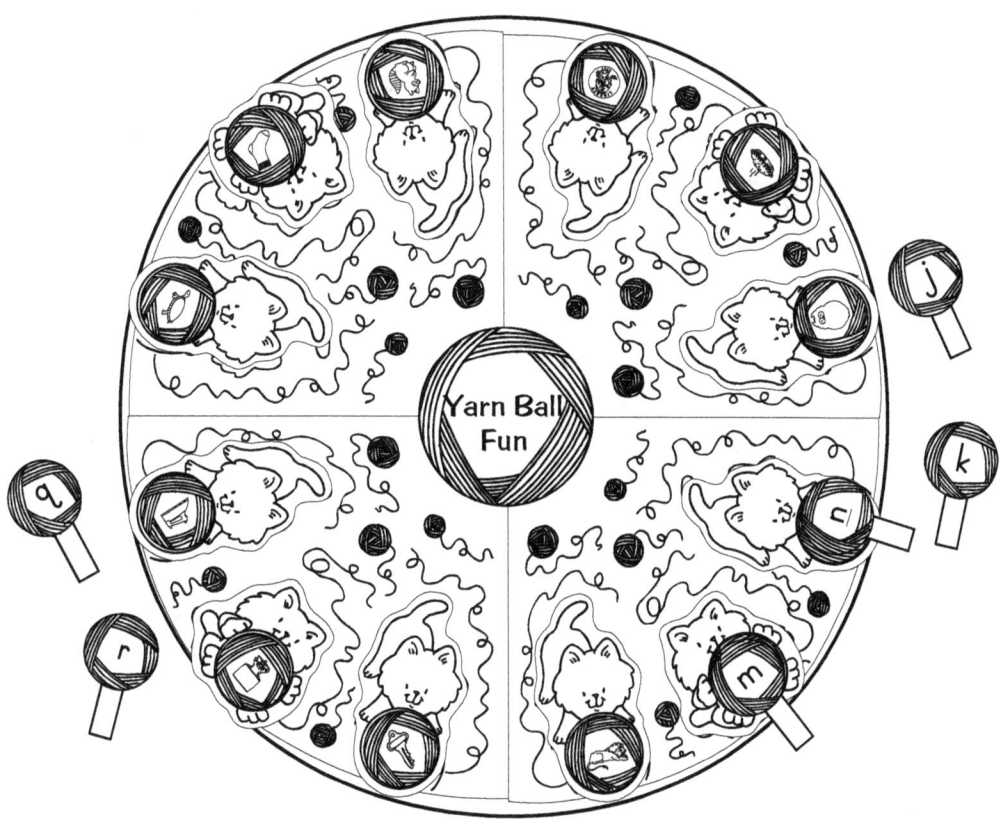

Materials
crayons, markers, scissors, glue, file folders, clothespins, large envelope

Assembly
Game Board: Reproduce, color, and cut out four game board patterns. Matching along the straight edges, glue the game board patterns on a poster board circle to form a round game board. Glue the title in the center of the game board. Reproduce two sets of kitten patterns. Reproduce, color, cut out, and glue an alphabet picture yarn ball game card on each kitten pattern. Then glue the kitten patterns around the game board. Note: Make additional game boards to provide skills practice for the entire alphabet.

Clothespin Game Cards: Reproduce, color, and cut out 12 lowercase letter game cards to match the alphabet pictures on the game board. Glue a clothespin to the back of each game card. Decorate a large envelope with yarn and kitten cutouts. Store the clothespin game cards in the envelope. (Include non-matching game cards for advanced players, or all matches for early learners.)

How to Play
Set up the game board on a table. Place the clothespin game cards, face down, on the table. Each player, in turn, draws a clothespin. If there is a match, the player identifies the match, and clips the clothespin to the correct kitten. If there is no match, the player places the clothespin back on the table, face down. Play continues until a clothespin is attached to each matching kitten on the game board.

Yarn Ball Fun Game Board and Title

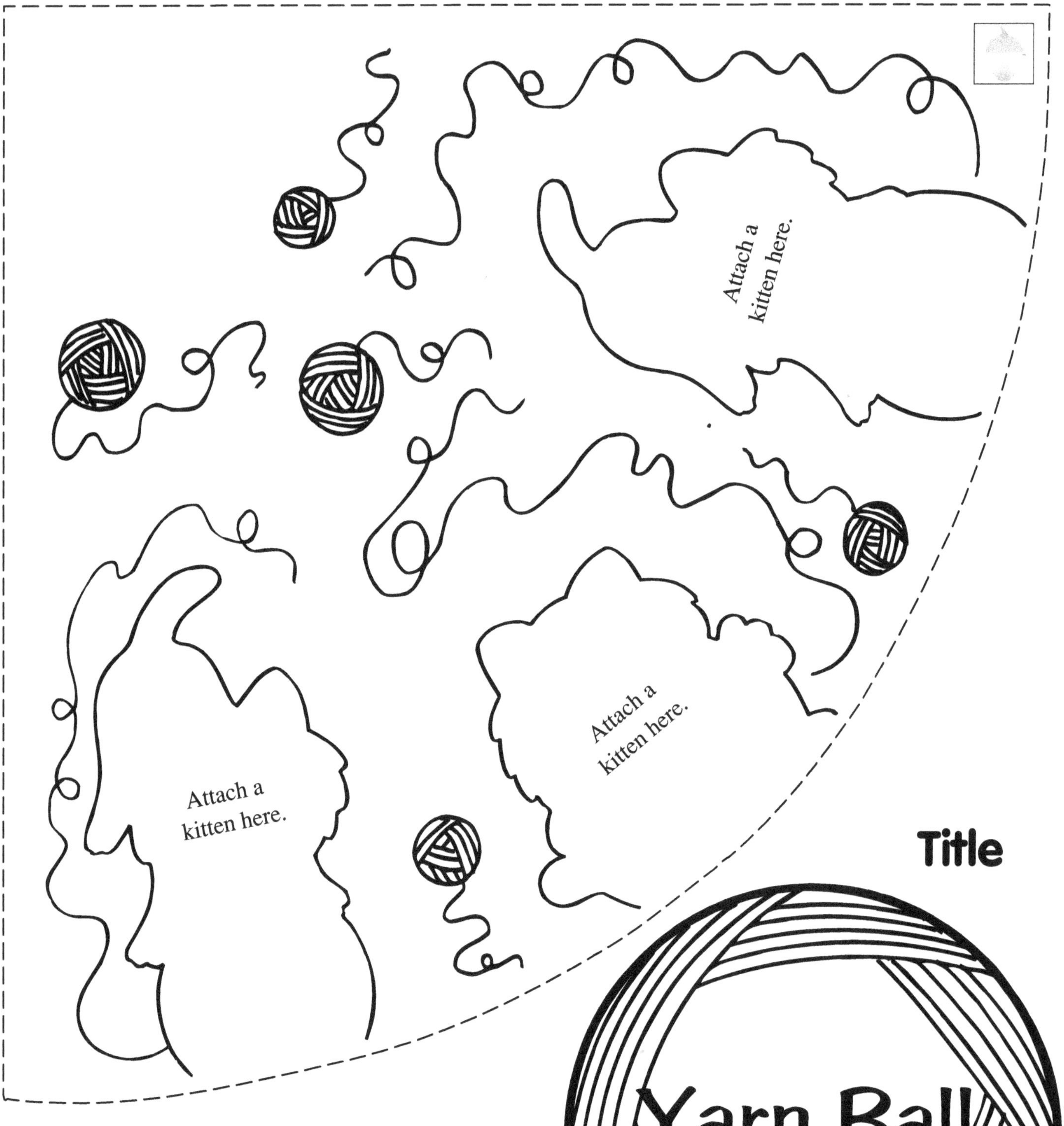

Attach a kitten here.

Attach a kitten here.

Attach a kitten here.

Title

Yarn Ball Fun

Reproduce, color, cut out, and assemble four game board patterns on a poster board circle to form a round game board. Glue the title in the center of the game board.

Kitten Patterns

Reproduce two sets of kitten patterns. Reproduce, color, cut out, and glue an alphabet picture yarn ball game card on each kitten pattern. Then glue the kitten patterns around an assembled Yarn Ball Fun game board.

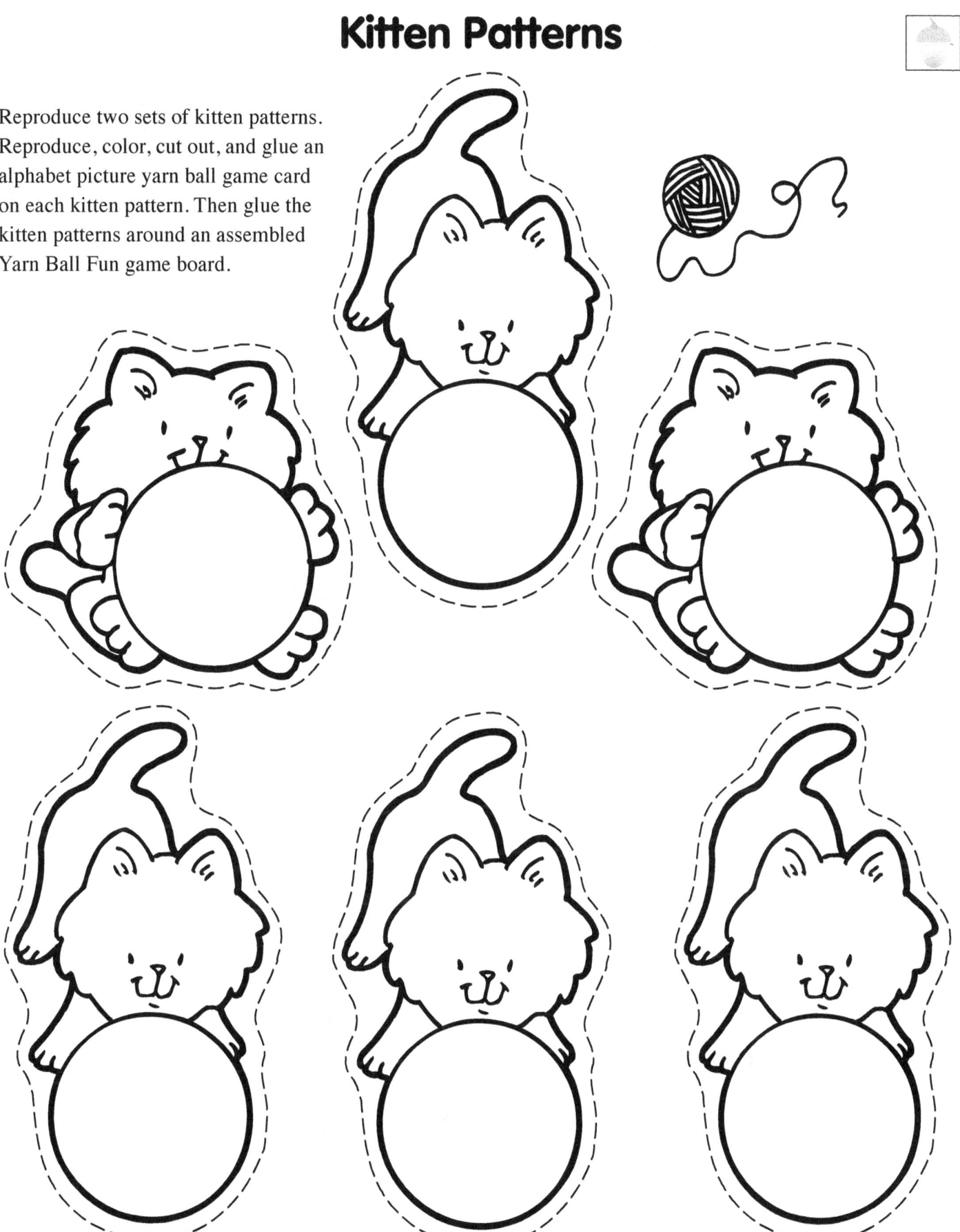

Creative Option: Reproduce a kitten pattern for each child to color and cut out. Have children glue large pom poms on the circles. Then glue each child's kitten to a paper cup for a pencil or crayon container.

Yarn Ball Game Cards

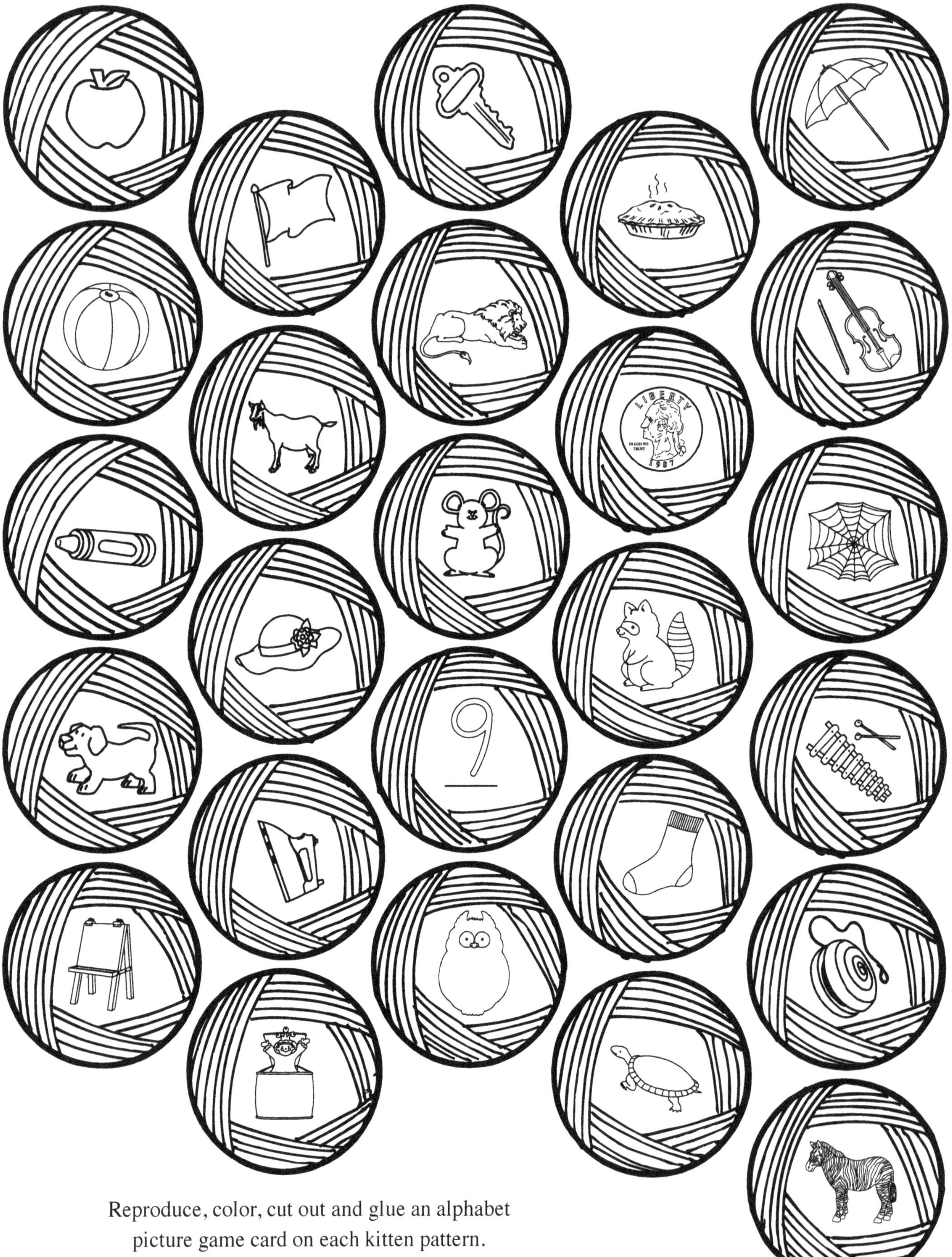

Reproduce, color, cut out and glue an alphabet picture game card on each kitten pattern.

Yarn Ball Game Cards

a k u
f p
b l v
g q
c m w
h r
d n x
i s
e o y
j t z

Reproduce, color, and cut out one set of yarn ball game cards. Glue a clothespin to the back of each game card.

LAB201310 • ALPHABET SOUP • 978-1-937257-45-3 • © 2014 Little Acorn Books™

Flower Power
A Clothespin Game
For Two Players

Materials
crayons, markers, scissors, glue, file folders, clothespins, large envelope

Assembly
Game Board: Reproduce, color, and cut out four game board patterns. Matching along the straight edges, glue the game board patterns on a poster board circle to form a round game board. Glue the title in the center of the game board. Reproduce two sets of flower patterns. Reproduce, color, cut out, and glue an uppercase letter game card on each flower pattern. Then glue the flower patterns around the game board. Note: Make additional game boards to provide skills practice for the entire alphabet. For alternate programming options see page 38.

Clothespin Game Cards: Reproduce, color, and cut out 12 lowercase letter game cards to match the uppercase letters on the game board. Glue a clothespin to the back of each game card. Decorate a large envelope with flower patterns. Store the clothespin game cards in the envelope. (Include non-matching game cards for advanced players, or all matches for early learners.)

How to Play
Set up the game board on a table. Place the clothespin game cards, face down, on the table. Each player, in turn, draws a clothespin. If there is a match, the player identifies the match, and clips the clothespin to the correct space. If there is no match, the player places the clothespin back on the table, face down. Play continues until a clothespin is attached to each matching space on the game board.

Flower Power Game Board and Title

Attach a flower pattern here.

Attach a flower pattern here.

Attach a flower pattern here.

Title

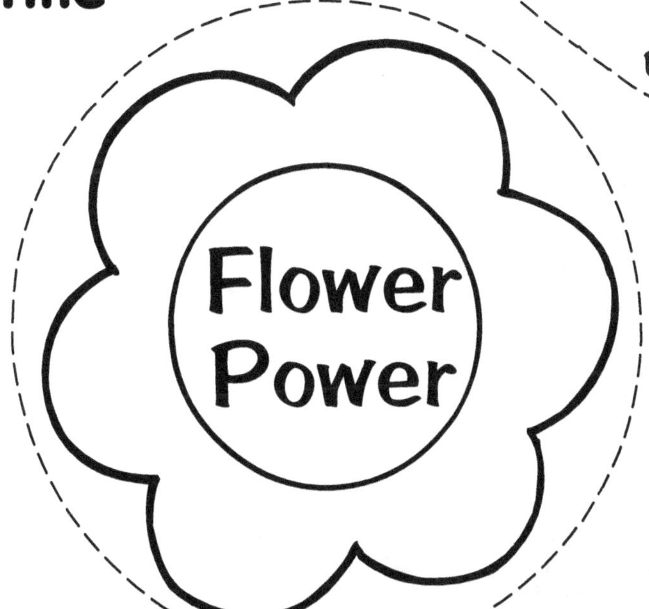

Flower Power

Reproduce, color, cut out, and assemble four game board patterns on a poster board circle to form a round game board. Glue the title in the center of the game board.

Flower Patterns

Reproduce two sets of flower patterns.
Reproduce, color, cut out, and glue an uppercase letter game card on each flower pattern.
Then glue the flower patterns around an assembled Flower Power game board.

Creative Option: Reproduce, color, and cut out the flower patterns. Glue craft tissue scraps, glitter, or pom poms to each flower. Tape a safety pin to the back of each flower to make a pin.

Flower Game Cards

A B C

D E F

G H I

J K L

M N O

Flower Game Cards

P Q R

S T U

V W X

Y Z

Reproduce, color, and cut out one set of flower game cards.

Creative Option: Make an alphabet bouquet. Reproduce, color, and cut out the flowers. Tape a plastic straw to the back of each flower. Place the flowers in a vase.

Flower Game Cards

a b c

d e f

g h i

j k l

m n o

Flower Game Cards

p	q	r
s	t	u
v	w	x
	y	z

Reproduce, color, and cut out one set of flower game cards.

Creative Option: Provide children with construction paper, letter flowers, and green yarn to make Alphabet Flower Gardens. Help each child cut and glue yarn stems and leaves on a sheet of construction paper. Then have children glue letter flowers at the top of each stem. Write each child's name on the back of his or her picture.

Flower Game Cards

Flower Game Cards

Reproduce, color, and cut out one set of game cards. Glue a clothespin to the back of each game card.

Programming Options:

- Program game boards with lowercase letter game cards. Then assemble alphabet picture clothespin game cards to match the lowercase letters on each game board.

- Assemble alphabet picture clothespin game cards to match game boards programmed with uppercase letters.

Strawberry Shortcake
A Match Board Game
For Two Players

Materials
crayons, markers, scissors, glue, file folder, envelope, bowl

Assembly
Game Board: Reproduce, color, and cut out the cover and two game board patterns. Glue each game board pattern to the inside of a folder. Reproduce, color, cut out, and glue five shortcake patterns on each game board. Glue the cover to the front of the folder, then laminate. Tape an envelope to the back of the game board folder to store game cards. Note: Make additional game boards to provide skills practice for the entire alphabet.

Game Cards: Reproduce, color, laminate, then cut out the strawberry game cards. Option: Reproduce, color, and glue the game cards page to the back of a sheet of gift wrap, then laminate and cut out the strawberries. Store the game cards in the envelope on the back of the game board folder. (Include non-matching strawberry game cards for advanced players, or all matches for early learners.)

How to Play
Set up the game board and cards on a table. Shuffle and place the strawberry game cards, face down, in a bowl. Each player, in turn, draws a card. If there is a match, the player identifies the match, and places the card on the correct shortcake. If there is no match, the player places the card, face down, in a discard pile. Play continues until every shortcake is topped with a matching strawberry card. Place discarded strawberry cards in the bowl if needed.

Strawberry Shortcake Cover

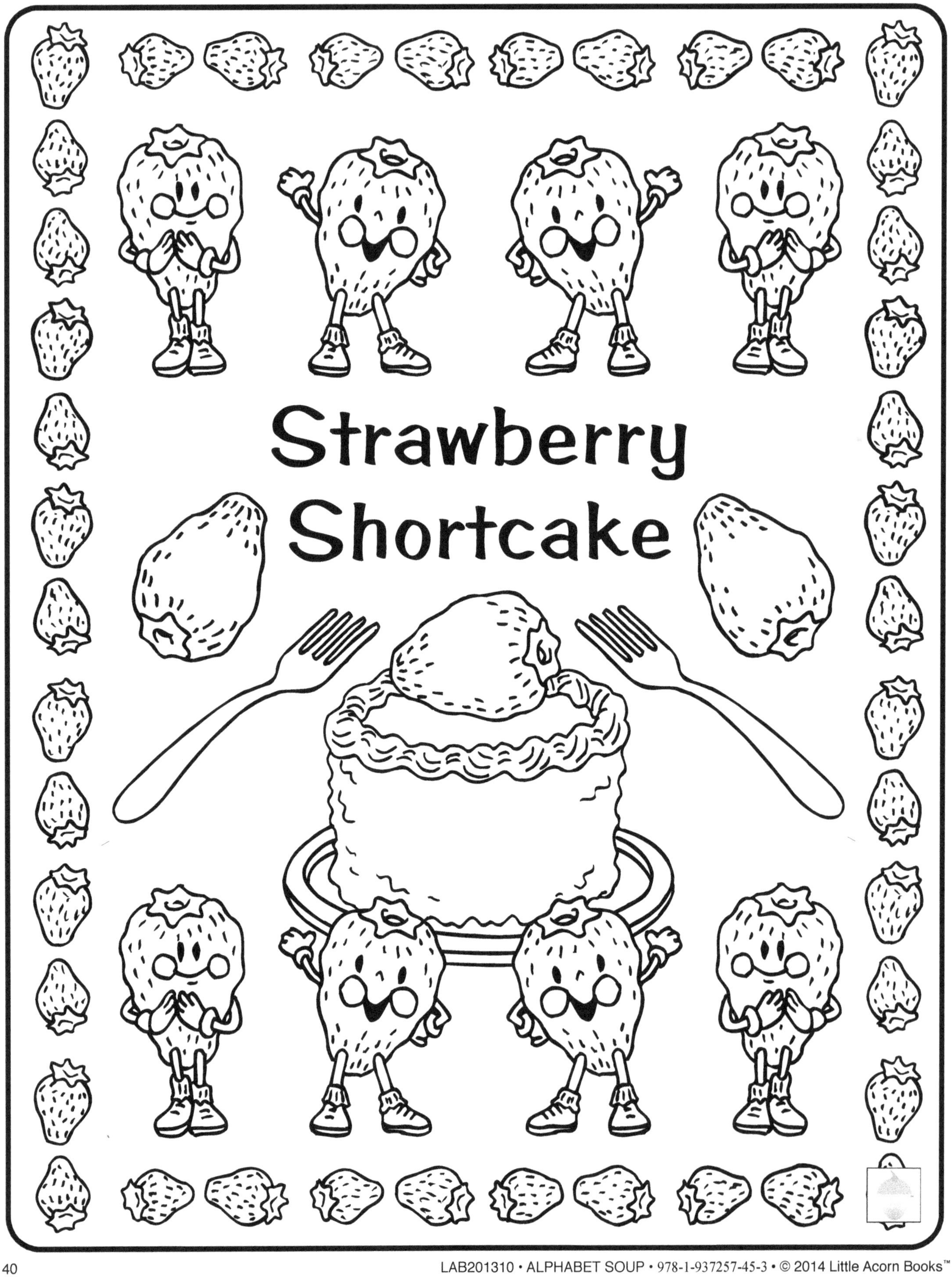

Strawberry Shortcake

Strawberry Shortcake Game Board

Strawberry Shortcake

Attach a shortcake pattern here.

Attach a shortcake pattern here.

Attach a shortcake pattern here.

Attach a shortcake pattern here.

Attach a shortcake pattern here.

Place a matching strawberry on each shortcake.

Shortcake Patterns

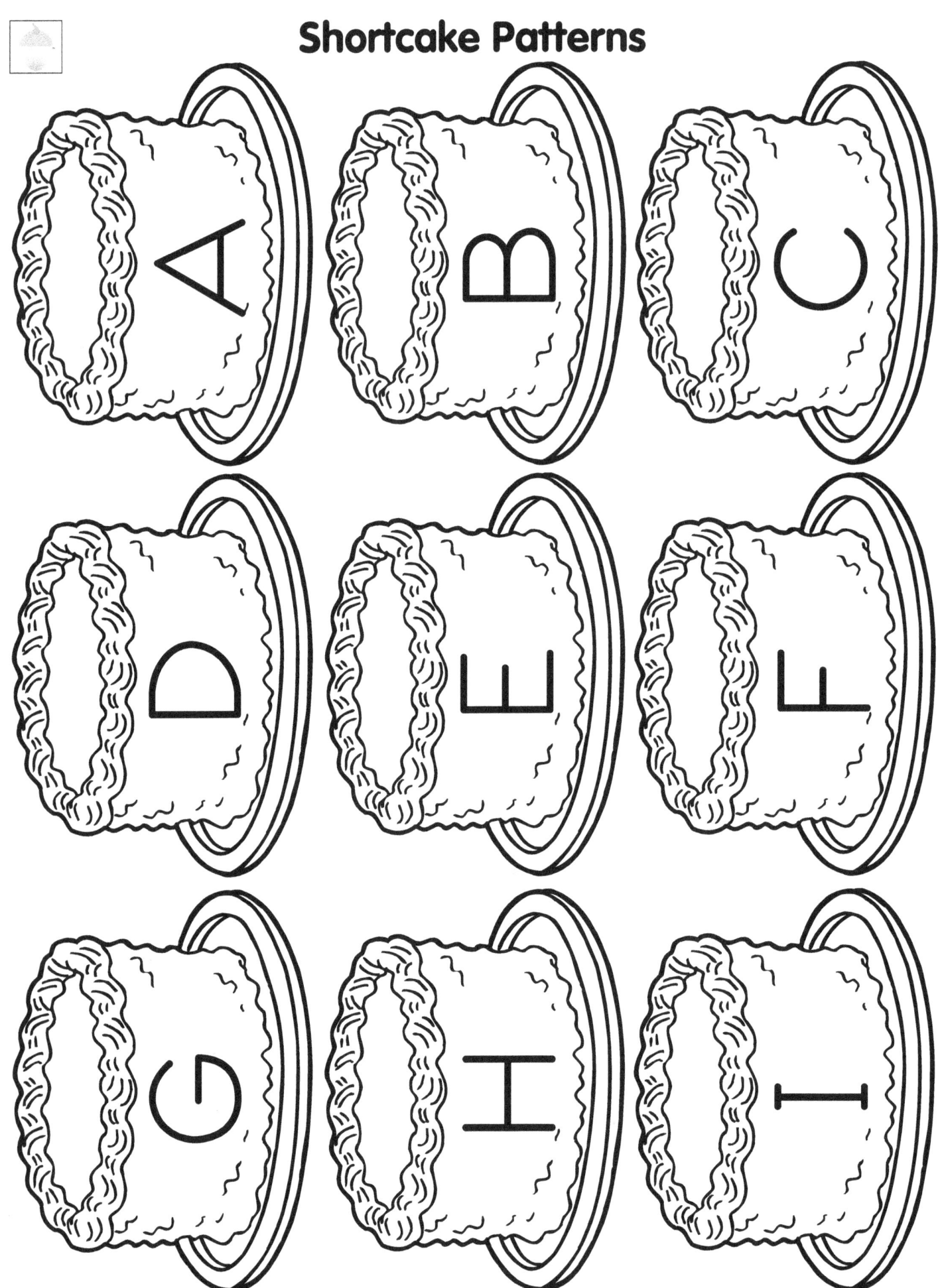

Shortcake Patterns

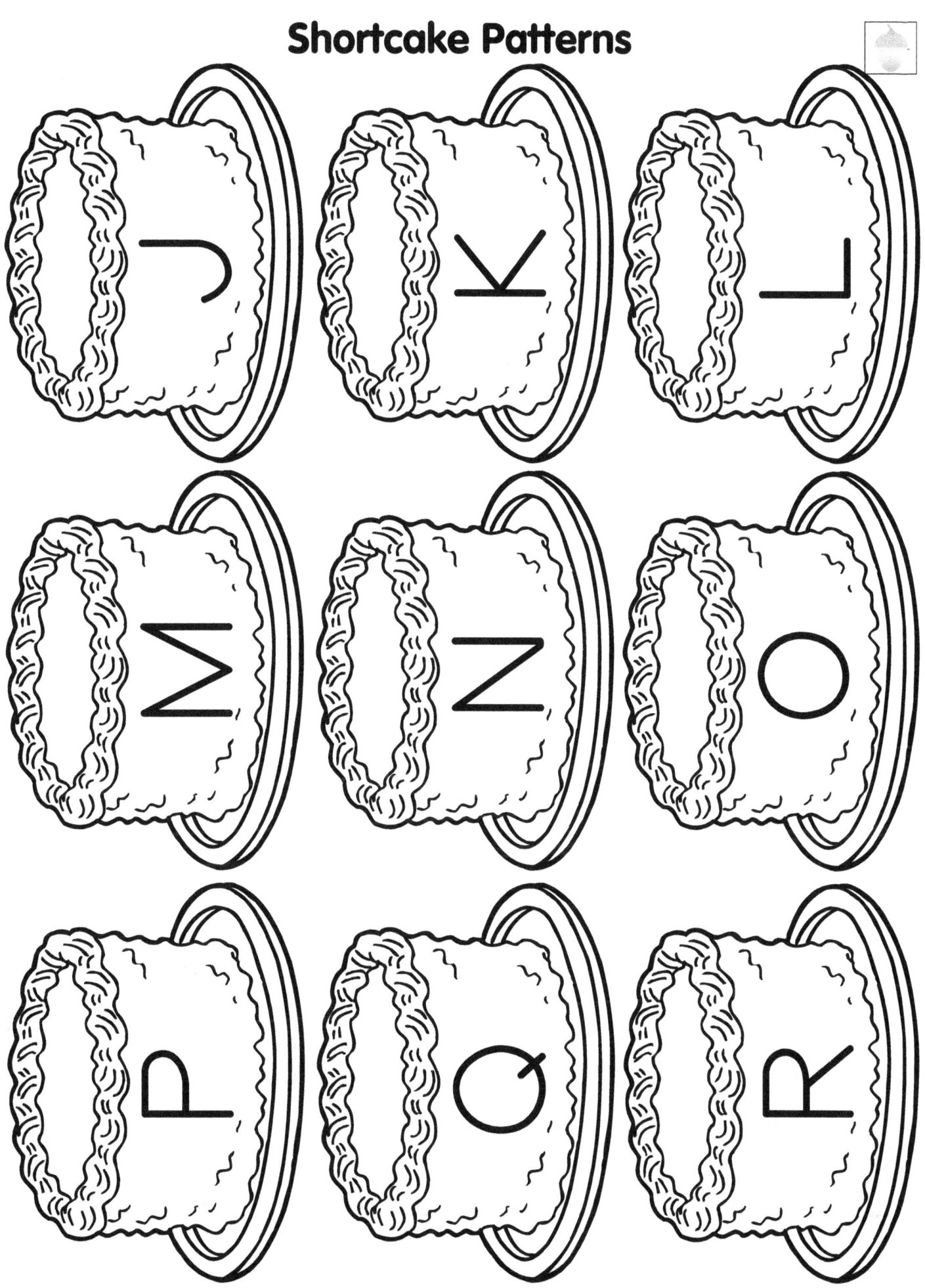

Shortcake Patterns

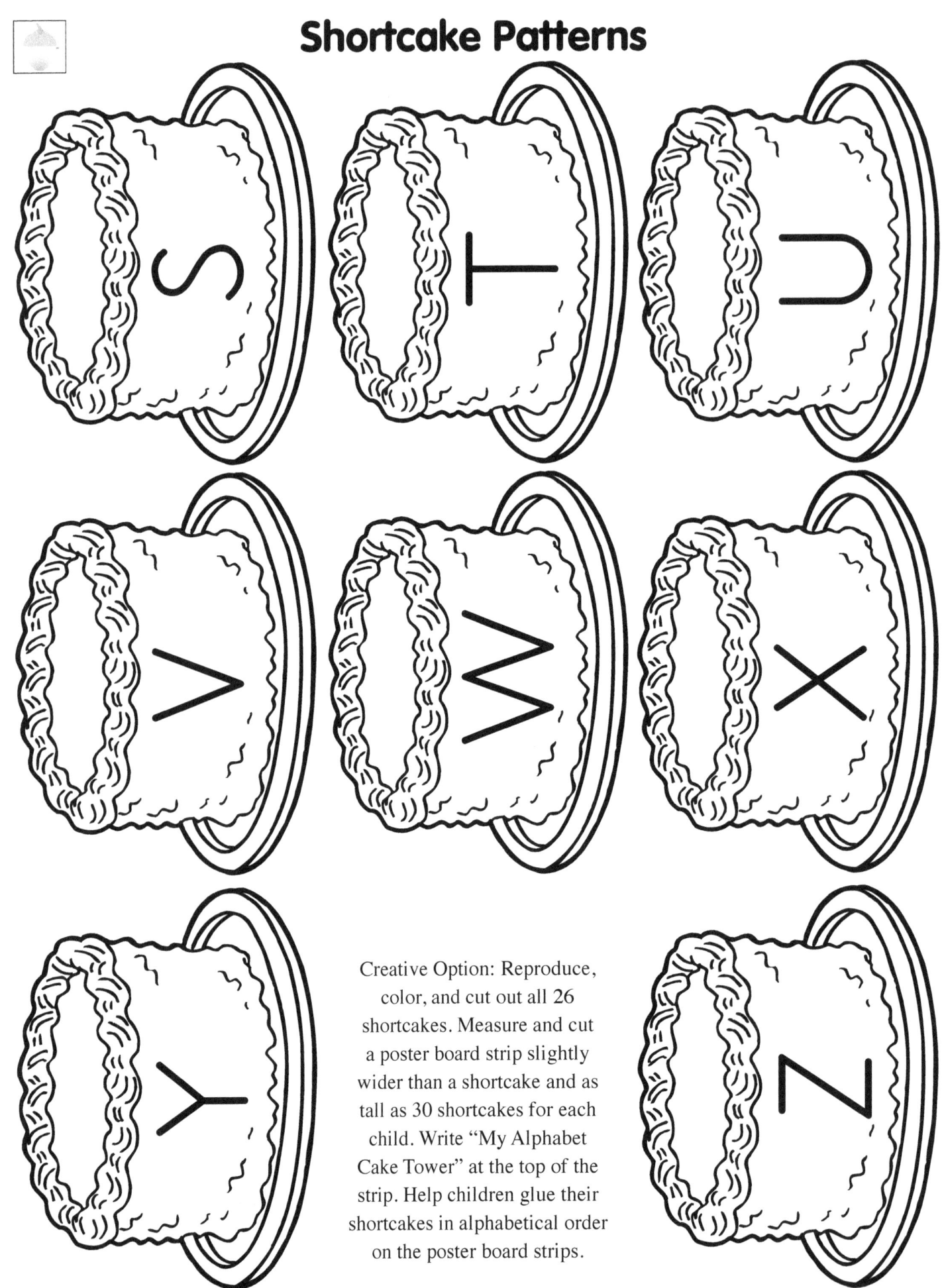

Creative Option: Reproduce, color, and cut out all 26 shortcakes. Measure and cut a poster board strip slightly wider than a shortcake and as tall as 30 shortcakes for each child. Write "My Alphabet Cake Tower" at the top of the strip. Help children glue their shortcakes in alphabetical order on the poster board patrips.

Strawberry Game Cards

a
b c
d e f
g h i j
k l m n
o p q r
s t u v
w x y z

Alphabet Bowling
A Match Board Game
For Two Players

Materials
crayons, markers, scissors, glue, file folder, envelope

Assembly
Game Board: Reproduce, color, and cut out the cover and two game board patterns. Glue each game board pattern to the inside of a folder. Reproduce, color, cut out, and glue ten bowling pin patterns on each game board. Glue the cover to the front of the folder, then laminate. Tape an envelope to the back of the game board folder to store game cards. Note: Make additional game boards to provide practice for the entire alphabet.

Game Cards: Reproduce, color, laminate, then cut out one set of bowling ball game cards. Option: Reproduce, color, and glue the game cards page to the back of a sheet of gift wrap, then laminate and cut out the bowling balls. Store the game cards in the envelope on the back of the game board folder. (Include non-matching bowling ball game cards for advanced players, or all matches for early learners.)

How to Play
Set up the game board on a table. Each player chooses a side of the board to play. One player shuffles and places the bowling ball game cards, face down, on the table. Each player, in turn, draws a card. If there is a match, the player identifies the match, and places the card on the correct bowling pin. If there is no match, the player places the card, face down, in a discard pile. Play continues until each player has placed a matching bowling ball on every bowling pin on his or her game board.

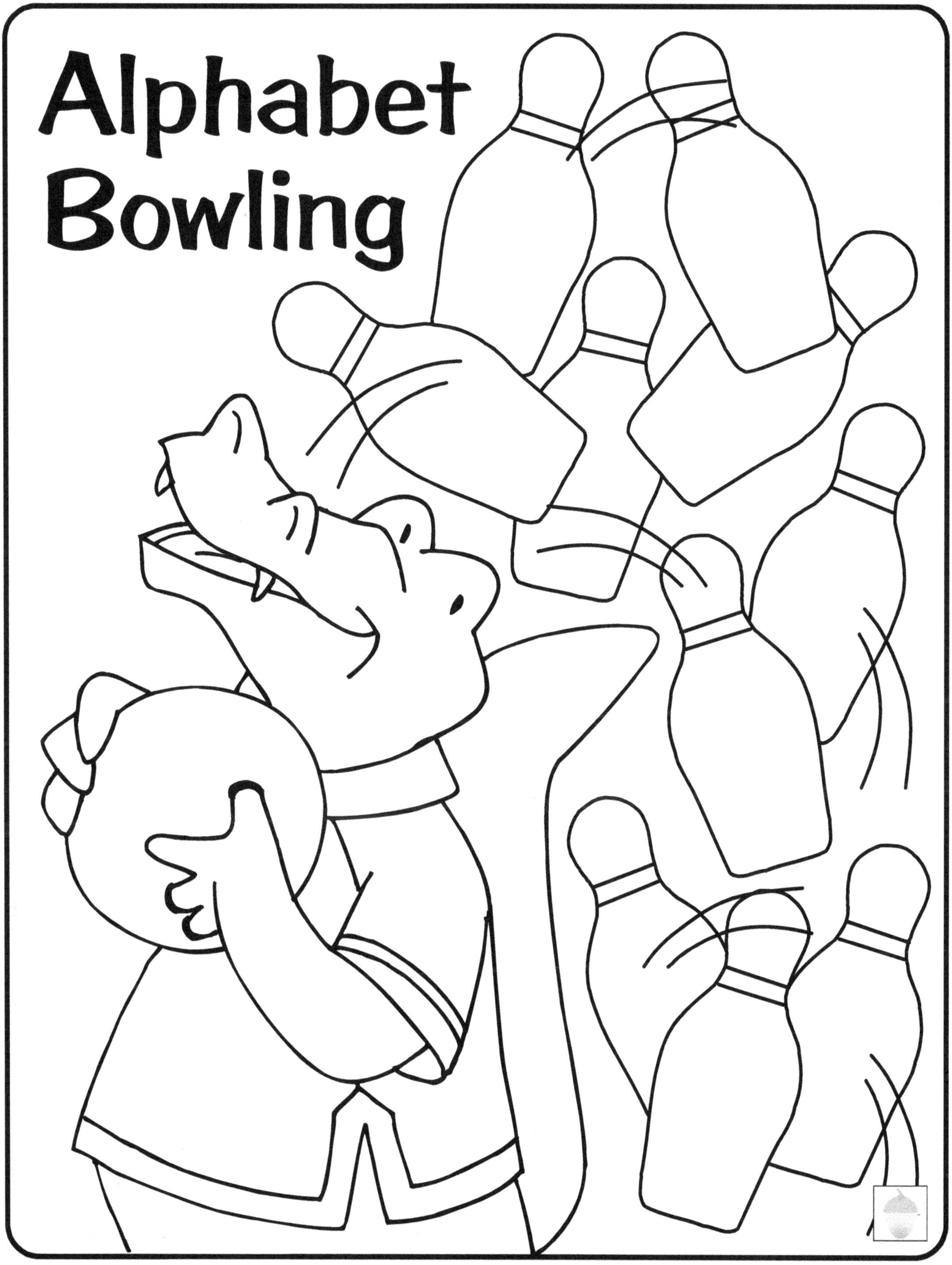

Alphabet Bowling Cover

Alphabet Bowling

Alphabet Bowling Game Board

Alphabet Bowling

Place a matching bowling ball on each bowling pin.

(10 bowling pin outlines labeled "Attach a bowling pin here.")

Bowling Pin Patterns

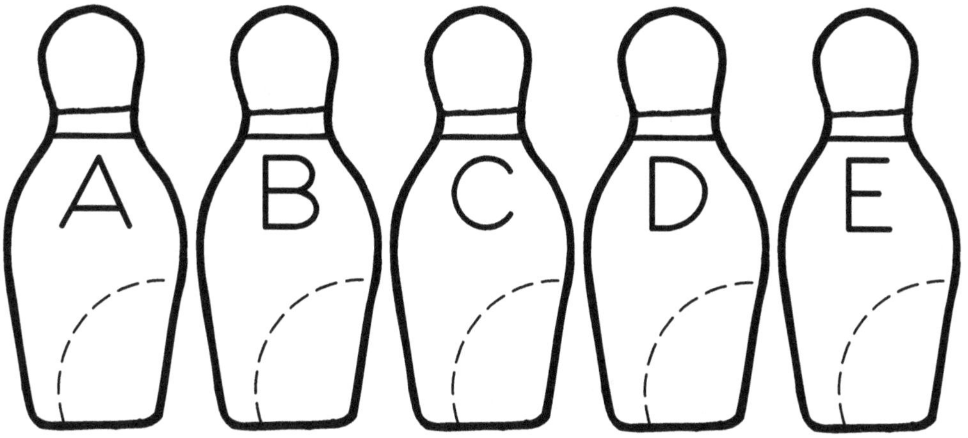

Reproduce, color, cut out, and glue ten bowling pin patterns on each game board.

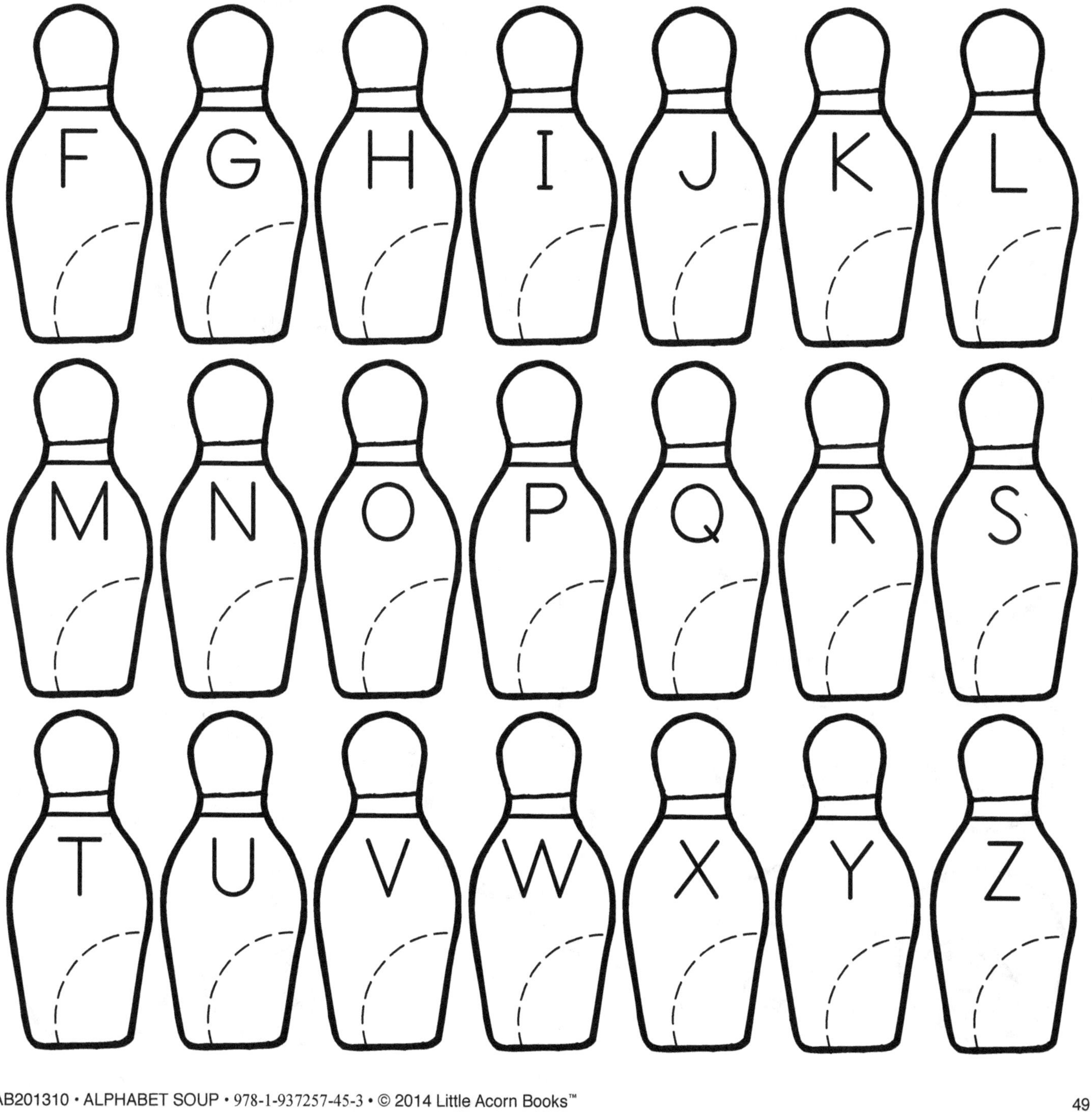

A B C D E
F G H I J K L
M N O P Q R S
T U V W X Y Z

Bowling Ball Game Cards

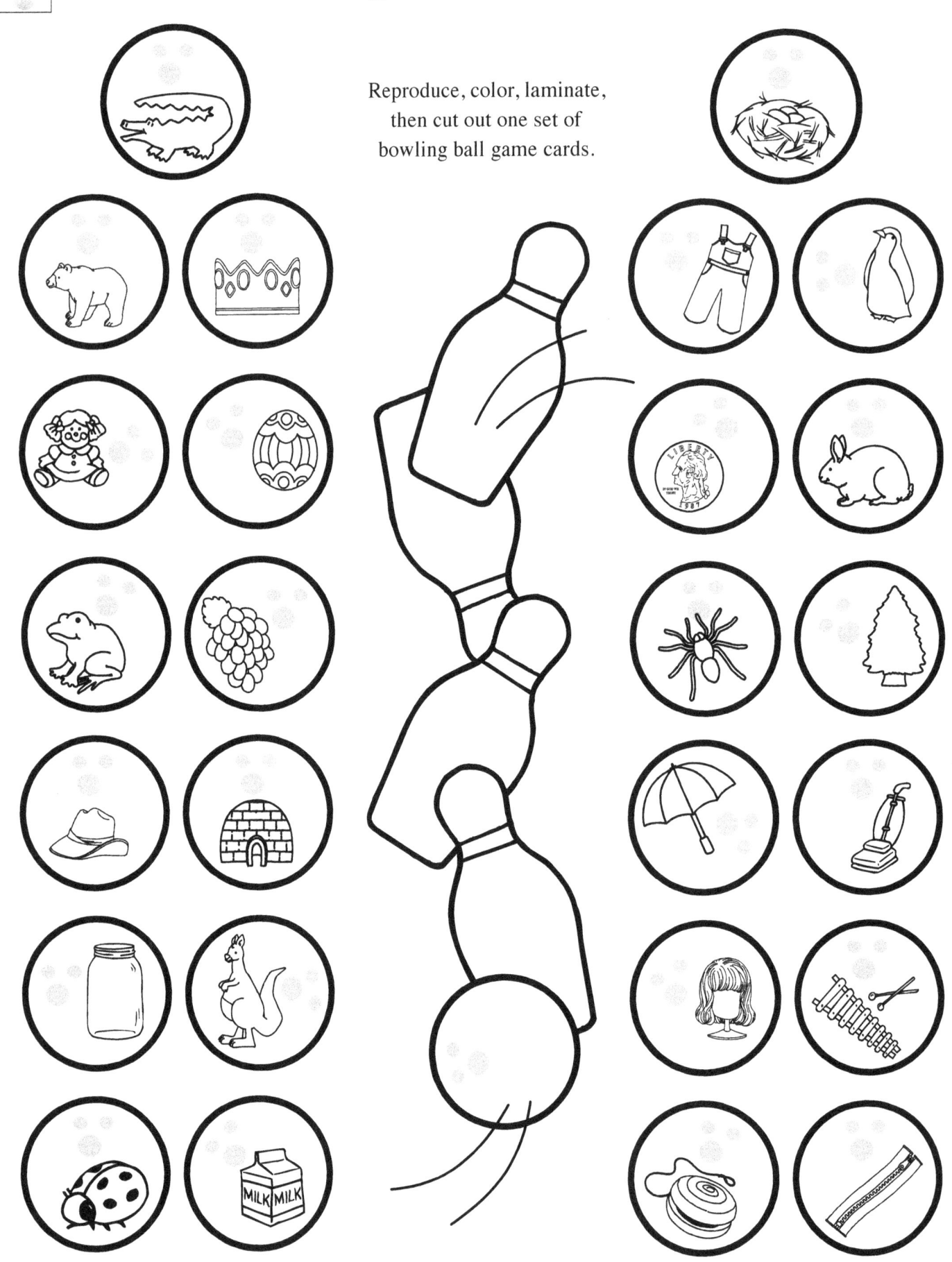

Reproduce, color, laminate, then cut out one set of bowling ball game cards.

Zoom Zoom
A Match Board Game
For Two Players

Materials
crayons, markers, scissors, glue, file folder, envelope, paper bag

Assembly
Game Board: Reproduce, color, and cut out the cover and two game board patterns. Glue each game board pattern to the inside of a folder. Reproduce, color, cut out, and glue five Martian patterns on each game board. Glue the cover to the front of the folder, then laminate. Tape an envelope to the back of the game board folder to store game cards. Note: Make additional game boards to provide practice for the entire alphabet.

Game Cards: Reproduce, color, laminate, then cut out one set of lowercase letter or alphabet picture tile game cards. Option: Reproduce, color, and glue the game cards page to the back of a sheet of gift wrap, then laminate and cut out the tiles. Store the game cards in the envelope on the back of the game board folder. (Include non-matching tile game cards for advanced players, or all matches for early learners.)

How to Play
Set up the game board on a table. Place the tile game cards in a paper bag. Each player, in turn, draws a card. If there is a match, the player identifies the match, and places the card on the correct space ship. If there is no match, the player places the card, face down, in a discard pile. Play continues until each player has placed a matching tile on every space ship on his or her game board. Place the discarded tile game cards back in the paper bag if needed.

Zoom Zoom Cover

Zoom Zoom Game Board

Zoom Zoom

Attach a Martian pattern here.

Attach a Martian pattern here.

Attach a Martian pattern here.

Attach a Martian pattern here.

Attach a Martian pattern here.

Place a matching tile on each space ship.

Martian Patterns

Reproduce, color, cut out, and glue five Martian patterns on each game board.

A   I
B   F   J
C   G   K
D   H   L
E   M

Martian Patterns

Creative Option: Provide children with Martian cutouts and colored construction paper shapes (triangles, circles, squares, ovals, and rectangles). Have children design and glue shapes and Martian cutouts on a sheet of construction paper to form space ships. Children can also draw stars and planets on their pictures.

Tile Game Cards

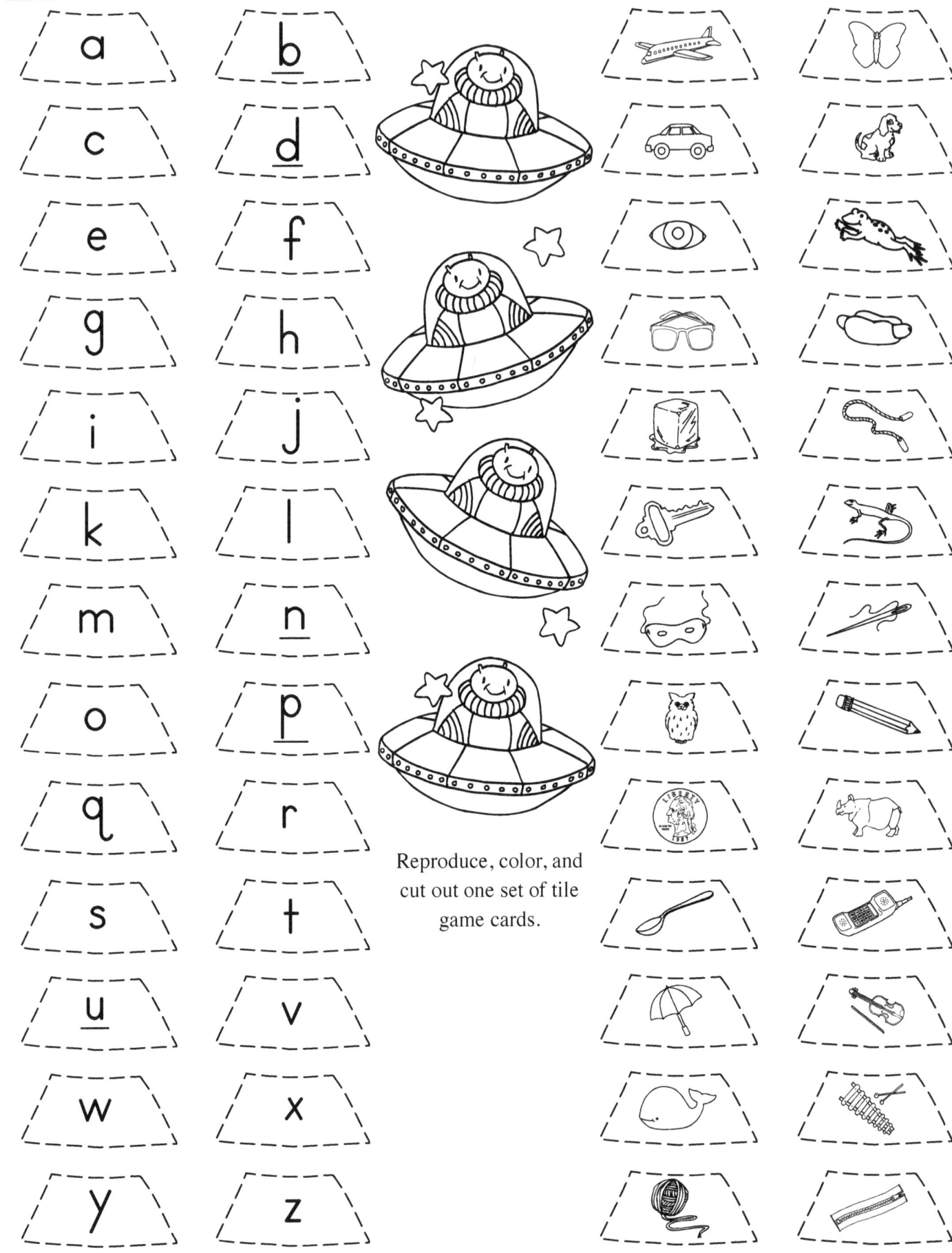

Reproduce, color, and cut out one set of tile game cards.

ABC Block Stackers
A Stacker Game
For One to Two Players

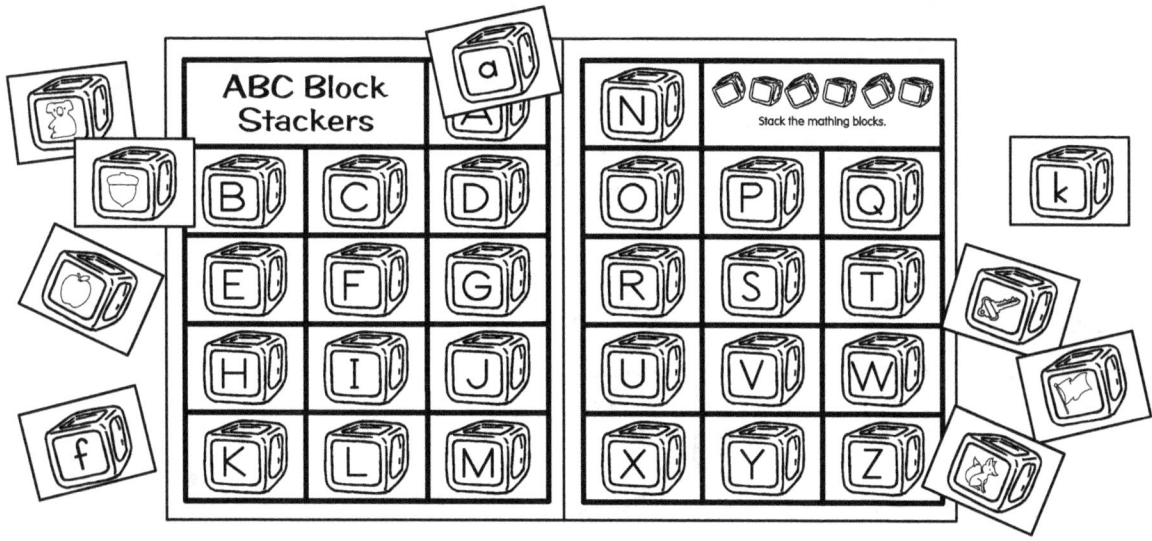

Materials
crayons, markers, scissors, glue, file folder, envelope

Assembly
Game Board: Reproduce, color, and cut out the block stackers game board patterns. Glue each game board pattern to the inside of a folder. Decorate the front of the folder with alphabet pictures from magazines or game card cutouts, then laminate. Tape an envelope to the back of the game board folder to store game cards.

Game Cards: Reproduce, color, laminate, then cut apart the game cards. Option: Reproduce, color, and glue each page of game cards to the back of a sheet of gift wrap, then laminate and cut apart the cards. Store the game cards in the envelope on the back of the game board folder.

How to Play
Set up the stacker game and cards on a table. One player shuffles and places the card deck, face down, on the table. Each player, in turn, draws, and stacks the drawn card on the matching space on the game board. Play continues until all the cards have been played.

Option: Use the game cards to play a game of Concentration. Shuffle and place all the cards, face down, on a table. Each player, in turn, turns over any two cards to find a match. If the player finds a match, he or she takes the cards and the next player takes a turn. If there is no match, each card is turned back over in the same position. Play continues until all the cards are taken.

ABC Block Stackers Game Board

ABC Block Stackers

A B C D E F G H I J K L M

ABC Block Stackers Game Board

Stack the matching blocks.

N		
O	P	Q
R	S	T
U	V	W
X	Y	Z

ABC Block Game Cards

ABC Block Game Cards

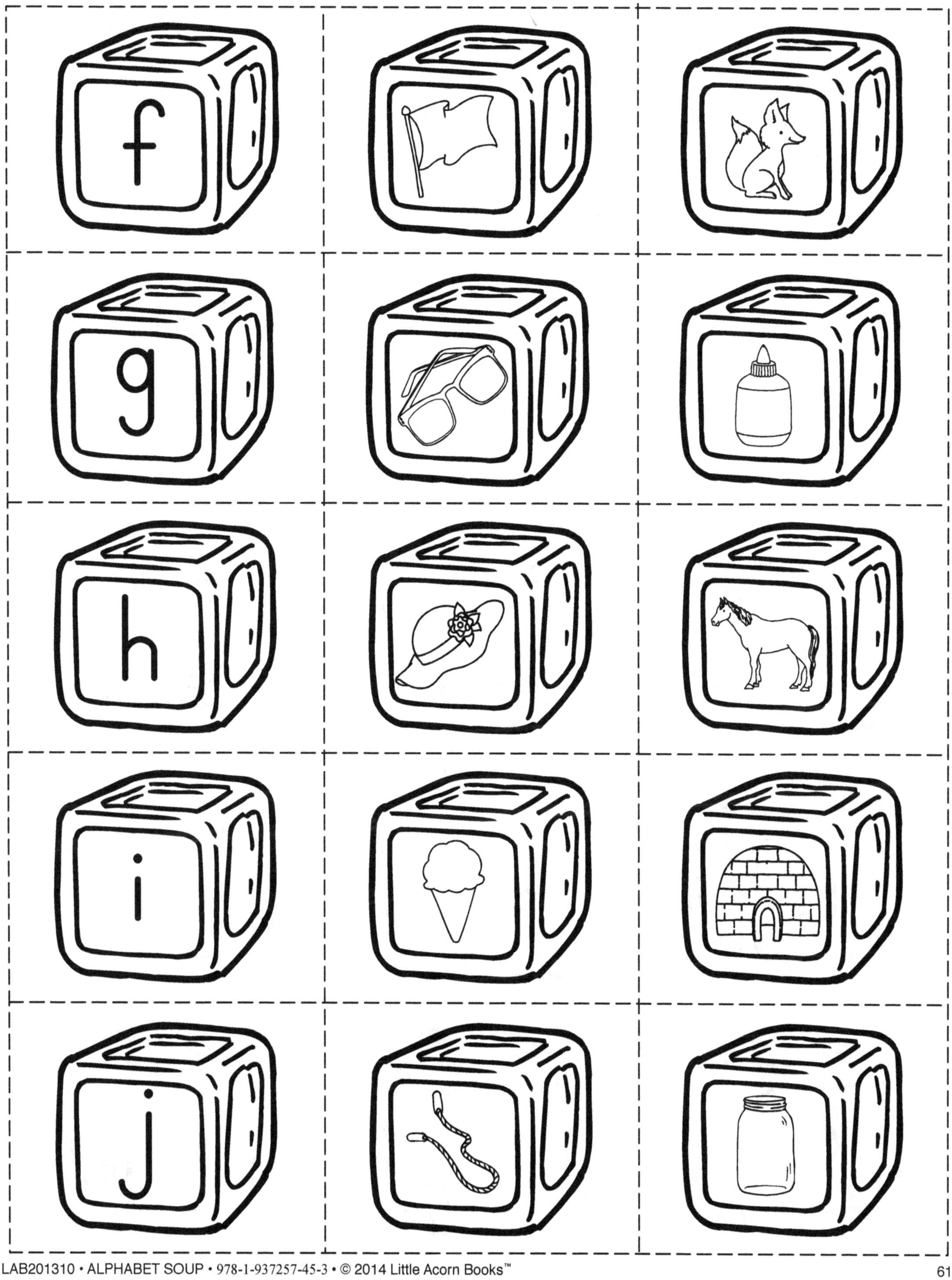

ABC Block Game Cards

ABC Block Game Cards

ABC Block Game Cards

Little Acorn Books™

Promoting Early Skills for a Lifetime™

A Hands-on Picture Book Series • Infancy–Age 4

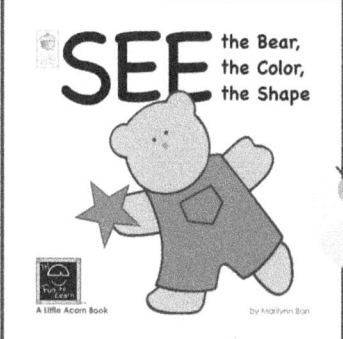

Miss Pitty Pat & Friends
Preschool–Grade 1

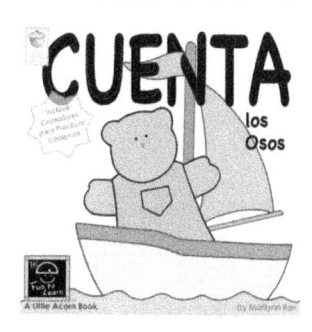

Using Crayons, Scissors, & Glue for Crafts
Preschool–Grade 1

Mookie's Christmas Tree
For All Ages and Not Just for Christmas

Little Acorn Books™
Visit our web site:
www.littleacornbooks.com

LAB201310 • ALPHABET SOUP • 978-1-937257-45-3 • © 2014 Little Acorn Books™

www.ingramcontent.com/pod-product-compliance
Lightning Source LLC
Chambersburg PA
CBHW081455060426
42444CB00037BA/3293